EVOLVE

THE PATH TO TRAUMA-INFORMED LEADERSHIP

Evolve: The Path to Trauma-Informed Leadership

YGTMedia Co. Trade Paperback Edition.

ISBN trade paperback: 978-1-998754-19-9

eBook: 978-1-998754-20-5

Published in Canada, for Global Distribution by YGTMedia Co.

www.ygtmedia.co/publishing

To order additional copies of this book: publishing@ygtmedia.co

Edited by Christine Stock

Interior design and typesetting by Doris Chung

Cover design by John Nethersole

eBook Conversion by Ellie Sipilä

Author Photo by Monique Hutson

All graphics used with permission.

TORONTO

EVOLVE

THE PATH TO TRAUMA-INFORMED LEADERSHIP

Carolyn Swora

FOREWORD BY GLAIN ROBERTS-MCCABE

Dedicated to my sons, Ayden and Andrew, who inspired me to look into deep, dark, scary places and let the sun shine in.

TABLE OF CONTENTS

FOREWORD

By Glain Roberts-McCabe

For close to thirty years now I've been leading teams. More than fifty if you count the fact that I'm the oldest of four kids and my brothers will tell you that I've been ordering them around since they showed up outside of our mother's womb.

For the first third of my leadership career, I stumbled blindly along, not really thinking about how I was impacting others (why are my direct reports driving me crazy?!). I found leadership stressful, daunting, and not very rewarding and tried to step out of it twice. But like a moth to a flame, I was lured back.

During the second third of my career, I had the good fortune to join a consultancy that focused on (among other things) leadership development.

There, I started the journey of understanding myself more as a leader. I went through the self-absorbed phase of being intrigued with my "special sauce" and became an assessment aficionado. I watched my Myers Briggs scores evolve over a decade and learned how my right-brain dominance made me innovative and quick thinking, how my Kolbe profile made me an expert improviser, and how my DiSC and colors profiles characterized me as a results driver who knew how to motivate those around me. I also learned that I have a driving motivational energy around winning AND independence. (Side note: That makes for a fun marriage. Ask my husband.)

I loved all my wonderful attributes from these tests and conveniently glossed over the less-than-charming aspects of each one. And then I got kicked in the teeth and came down to earth when I did my first 360 review. It was through that process that I was faced with the uncomfortable discovery that it wasn't my direct reports that were the problem, it was me. Of course, the usual anger (try and walk a mile in my shoes!), denial (I'm not THAT bad!), and ultimately acceptance (do I want to improve or do I want to be right?) followed.

I dug deep into coaching in the early 2000s and cried my way through my training program. At the time, I thought the tears were of frustration because of the job I was in, the pressure I was feeling as a senior leader, and the fact that my freedom of choice had rapidly shifted with the responsibilities that came with marriage and home ownership. Looking back on that time now, I realize I was a powder keg of emotion that was unconsciously being perpetually shoved down into a box.

One night around that time I lay in bed with my husband, talking through an issue that was happening at work, and he calmly said to me, "I think you should examine your relationship with control."

Did I mention my husband is a social worker (now psychotherapist)?

I've been thinking about that statement for more than twenty years. And it's only since facing my trauma that I've been able to unlock the answer to that provocation.

Because I'm a coach married to a psychotherapist, there have been many debates and discussions in our house of the relevance of past experiences. Why retrench history that you can't change? What's the point in going back into painful moments when you can focus on moving forward? This was me. On repeat. As a perpetual optimist (I was once told that I was optimistic to the point of delusion), I have a deep dislike of discomfort and will do everything imaginable to avoid it. Therapy has always been a convenient scapegoat.

Like many of us, I had a difficult childhood. My father was domineering and physically and emotionally abusive, but he was also doing the best he could with the skills he was given. To label my upbringing as "traumatic" seemed over the top. Dramatic even.

Challenging? Sure. Painful. Absolutely. But traumatic? Let's not go overboard.

And yet, as I sit in the third and possibly final chapter of my leadership career, I find myself four years on in a journey of being able to acknowledge the trauma that occurred in my life and how it's affected both my personal and work relationships. It's this insight that has helped me start to answer my husband's provocation about my relationship with control.

Grow up in a family with a controlling father and, for me, a couple of things happened:

- I never wanted to be in a situation where anyone would control me again—from bosses to partners to employees.
- I felt a huge sense of responsibility to buffer my brothers and mother from my father's moods. I took on the role of running interference by being hyper-vigilant. This hypervigilance means I take responsibility for too many things and also get frustrated when other people foist responsibility on me ("What's for dinner?" is one of my least favorite questions of all time!).

So, I get snappy when I feel like my partner, daughter, team or [fill in the blank] is putting too much on my plate and/or if they're not stepping up to take responsibility for things quickly enough (gotta move fast before Dad gets mad!). I feel constricted when people try to help me and uncomfortable leaning on others. Delegation of tasks is okay for me but delegation of emotional support / being vulnerable? Way more difficult.

See, that's the thing about trauma. It sits with you whether you choose to acknowledge it or not. It sets your patterns. It drives your beliefs. It is your unconscious copilot for good or bad. And when you finally take a deep breath and shine the light on your trauma, you are never not able to see it again.

With a wider view of yourself and your patterns, you're given the gift of being able to make new and different choices.

Over the past twenty-five years, I've had the opportunity to work with thousands of leaders. Specifically, our niche at my company The Roundtable is with leaders that organizations tend to label "high potentials," "high value," "key talent." No matter the industry, sector, functional area or level, one thing I've learned about leadership is this: it's situational and the very best leaders are able to combine self-insight with the know-how to adapt their approach to the situation at hand.

A situation might be a change in strategy, an uncertain economy, a new boss, a big promotion, or, most recently, a global pandemic. COVID-19 was a leadership situation in which some leaders excelled and others faltered. Those who excelled knew how to dial up their empathy, prioritize self-care, and build spaces where team members felt safe and heard.

As leaders look beyond the pandemic, we are facing the fallout of a collective trauma that we likely won't know the effects of for years or even decades to come. We've already seen glimpses of the power shifting between employer and employee and the old military/heroic model of leadership transitioning to a more collective, connected approach. For some, the changes we're facing will be easy to adapt to. For others, it will be very difficult. For everyone, it will require an open mind and an increased commitment to understanding and addressing the effects of work on mental health.

Five years ago, when the phrase "trauma-informed leadership" started creeping into my LinkedIn feed, I rolled my eyes. "Isn't leadership hard enough?!" I grumbled to myself. "Now you need me to be a flipping psychologist?!" Perhaps you feel the same.

But here's what I know for sure: the best thing you can do for the people you lead is to work on yourself.

In *Evolve*, Carolyn Swora debunks the idea that being trauma-informed means becoming a trauma therapist. *Evolve* provides an accessible primer on a difficult but important topic that will, at the very least, reframe your definition of trauma, and at the best, inspire you to develop your leadership practice to even deeper levels. For those of you brave enough to understand and label your own trauma, there is no doubt in my mind that the reward will be a richer, happier, more fulfilled life for yourself and for those around you.

As we all learn how to navigate life in an increasingly uncertain world, we owe it to ourselves and our teams to do all we can to level-up our leadership. The world is increasingly complex, the pressures on leaders relentless, and the need to make the unconscious conscious is critical if we are going to evolve our workplaces. By unpacking the parts of ourselves that need to be healed, we can be more intentional with our leadership, navigate changing situations more effectively, and move our teams, organizations, communities, and families forward with more clarity, compassion, and kindness. Each of us has the opportunity to be the leader who changes someone's life for the better, and the best place to start is with ourselves. Enjoy this journey.

INTRODUCTION

Bang. Bang. Bang. I was knocking as hard as I could on the apartment door. No answer. Again, I pounded my nine-year-old fist, desperate for my dad to open up. I didn't want to involve anyone else, but if he didn't answer soon, I was going to be left with no choice. Deep down I felt a pang of fear, but there was no time for that. The little warrior in me jumped into action.

I turned toward the elevator and waited. It gave me time to test a few scenarios in my head. I had to choose one that wouldn't raise the suspicion of the building superintendent, but it had to be one that would get him to unlock the door without asking too many questions.

Navigating a tricky situation like this with my dad was nothing new for me, and before long, I was back in the apartment. I fibbed to the superintendent and said my dad wasn't feeling well and was sleeping in the bedroom. The truth was, he had passed out, forgetting to leave the door unlocked.

My mom left my dad when I was three years old. I was their only child. It was the seventies, and my mom was advised by a lawyer that getting full custody of me would be incredibly difficult and expensive. They agreed that he would make reasonable child support payments and I would visit him every second weekend. My mom followed through, but he didn't.

This laid the foundation for my beliefs about leadership. Be strong, work hard, please others at all costs, and don't rock the boat. It served me well in my younger years, as I was a good student, a great athlete, and I sought leadership roles at school and in the community.

It only made sense then, as I entered into the grown-up phase of life and started my career, that I relied on these beliefs to be successful in the corporate world. Busyness and productivity were alluring, they brought results, and I was rewarded nicely for them. My future looked bright, and I felt invincible; I was able to handle anything that came my way.

And then life threw me a curve ball, one that would test everything I had learned about adversity.

I found out that my husband of one short year had metastatic stage 4 renal cell carcinoma, a prognosis that even the most professional of medical doctors struggle to share. The first symptom was blood in his urine, and thankfully, his family physician ran a bunch of tests instead of dismissing it as an infection. It was a short wait to find out the devastating news.

The ultrasound showed a giant mass on his left kidney. He had surgery soon after and took several weeks to recover. Our days were filled with hospital visits, appointments with oncologists and nephrologists, scans and tests, planning treatment, and hoping for the best. No one had admitted it was terminal, but I could see it in the doctors' reactions. The literature wasn't reassuring either: fewer than 10 percent of patients survived beyond a few years.

I was six months' pregnant when this happened. From the very moment of diagnosis, I knew that I would have to find the strength to carry our family and get us through it. Paul likely wouldn't live to see his children graduate from high school, let alone kindergarten.

I wasn't unfamiliar with shouldering the weight of emotional burdens. So, weirdly, I wasn't as scared as you might expect. I had mastered the tactics of perfection and perseverance by living through the emotional turbulence with my dad.

I doubled down on my coping mechanisms. I overcompensated for the lack of certainty by throwing myself even further into my work. I overperformed as much as I could. Performance felt good. It felt safe. Performance was rewarded; it was the easiest alternative to *feeling*. The most obvious alternative to vulnerability. I signed up for extra projects. I tried to be more domestic at home. I stepped in when anyone else, at home or work, needed help. As long as I was helpful, I could feel the sweetness of gratitude and reward without needing to deal with the rest. I needed as much as possible to be a sure thing, to be under control.

I did my best to be a loving wife and caregiver, a doting mom to two boys, and a productive super-star employee. Trips to the hospital were weekly. I'd pack up the stroller, diaper bag, and lots of snacks. The boys and I would visit the nurses while Daddy got his treatment. It was heartwarming to see the smiles and laughs our boys brought into the chemotherapy unit. These were moments of joy that I tried to focus on. But the fact was, toddlers are tiring, and caring for a dying spouse is tiring. I was too exhausted to realize that what I was living through was traumatic.

In January 2009, Paul passed away. He was thirty-eight. I was thirty-six. We were married for seven years. Cancer was an uninvited partner that just wouldn't leave and wreaked havoc for six of those years.

The only way I knew how to cope with it was to charge forward and to be tough and not complain, believing that the pain and weight I was carrying could disappear. I didn't realize that the trauma, a word I didn't know yet, had infiltrated my body and nervous system. In fact, it had been there since childhood.

WHEN ADAPTING LEADS TO BURNOUT

While I know my story may seem sad, I also know that it isn't entirely unique. The unfortunate reality is that all of us experience some kind of trauma in our lives. It might be a result of having an alcoholic parent or going through a painful divorce. It could be from living in an abusive home or simply experiencing repeated misunderstandings. A diagnosis. A *mis*diagnosis. A *missed* diagnosis. It could be from the loss of a friend or a great love. A miscarriage or redundancy. We will all meet grief; that's a simple fact of life. But trauma isn't limited to tragic events or situations like this. Trauma can also be an accumulation of smaller, less pronounced events. People will experience traumas, big and small, as part of human life. The only thing that's really certain is that we will experience lows at some point in our lives.

As humans, we are very resilient, intelligent, and capable, naturally adapting our behaviors to meet life's challenges. The problem is, these adaptations can turn into unhealthy coping mechanisms with long-term unhealthy consequences.

What I thought was ambition and tenacity were repeating patterns fooling me into thinking I was resilient. In actuality, they were constricting my voice, my authenticity, and my passion. I suffered through depression and burnout, yet I still spun unconsciously on repeat in a drive for corporate success.

I know I'm not alone since burnout is recognized by the World Health Organization as an occupational phenomenon.[1] This was before the COVID-19 pandemic, and from what I can see, it's only getting worse. The combination of traumatic events and an oppressive system masking itself as a meritocracy leaves us myopic and unable to see the big picture. In the focus to succeed, we can overlook the headwinds that propel some and tailwinds that oppress others. So many people are stuck on a hamster wheel and don't even know it, let alone know how to get off it.

I hope you contemplate your own hamster wheel as you read these pages.

LET'S BE HONEST, LEADERSHIP IS BROKEN

In my role as a culture and leadership consultant, I hear directly from clients about their challenges at work. As the days of the pandemic grew, I heard more panic and concern from leaders. People were burning out, being overrun by anger, harboring resentment, and appearing disconnected, and some were even identifying emotions like rage, sadness, or grief. Divisiveness and incivility that were once not tolerated were beginning to snowball. People were operating in ways that didn't feel reflective of who they really were, but they were unable to find a way out of the chaos.

That was me. I could see myself in every one of these stories. I could also see the research and data.

When we overlay the collective trauma that the pandemic created, it became the crack that broke the dam at work. We could no longer hide our past traumas or pretend our stress responses were just from "not having enough coffee yet." Report after report shared how people were looking at their relationship with work, with money, with achievement, with themselves—and feeling dissatisfied. They had learned from working under the pressures of the pandemic and weren't willing to go back to "normal." People have now realized that pre-pandemic levels of productivity were never "normal," and they believe that there's nothing for us to go back to because everything is different.

As leaders, we need to come to terms with this new reality and learn to lead differently. To lead more humanly. To accept that adversity is a fact of life and that we must be prepared to lead our people as if we understand that. It's not enough to "teach new behaviors" or simply attend training. You can't just read this book and consider that to be enough. It's been a long time coming, and collectively, we've been dancing around the idea that perhaps our leadership style is broken. Or, at the very least, our understanding of what it really means to be a great leader.

It's time to be blunt. Profound changes are needed in leadership.

To help us collectively evolve our workplaces from the inside out, it starts with us first—as leaders in organizations. When we go first, we give everyone around us permission to do the same. That's what leadership is.

Each of us has experienced trauma to some degree, in varying forms and intensity. It might be from challenges in your past. And without question, the pandemic has inflicted trauma on each of us. It's changed everything completely, even if we aren't yet aware of it; even if we feel we've come through it relatively unscathed.

This is the conversation I want to have with you. I want to talk about trauma and how its impact needs to reshape how we interact at work and the skills leaders now need to have in their toolbox. Burnout is no longer an option. We can't ignore the reality, like I did for so many years, that to be human is to have trauma. We now have no choice but to learn how to lead with an understanding of how it impacts us and the way we show up. The pandemic and its aftereffects have left us with nowhere to hide.

There are really only two ways to lead:

1. Tell people how to do things better.
2. Inspire people to figure out their own ways of doing things better.

Most people tend to fail on the second one, which is a shame because that's the only way to lead effectively. And this is why leadership is broken.

Throughout history and in all our studies of great leaders, our primary focus has been on what the leader does and the actions they take. It seems logical. However, the true sign of great leadership is great self-leadership. It is with a very sharp sense of self and a deepened awareness of all our parts, both good and bad and light and dark—it is the acceptance of who we are, the wholeness of who we really are, that allows us to step into the greatest version of ourselves. When we can do this, we give other people permission to do the same.

I like the idea of a world where we all have permission to be and accept and own and love who we really are. This is why trauma-informed leadership is nonnegotiable. It's not about fixing people. Trauma-informed leaders understand that people aren't broken, themselves included. They understand that they have trauma and will struggle, responding with compassion and empathy. They seek connection as a pathway through imperfection. They learn that in connection, there is safety that opens the door to creativity, innovation, and meaningful collaboration—all the elements of healthy workplace cultures that underpin successful business performance.

My hope with introducing this concept of trauma-informed leadership is twofold:

- It motivates you to explore your own reactivity and encourages you to find help to process it with a professional. Each of us needs to take ownership for identifying and processing the traumas in our lives—it's not up to other people or organizations to solve this for us. As we'll discuss, there is work organizations need to do, but repairing our individual trauma isn't it.
- Being trauma-informed is an understanding that your behaviors, regardless of intention, make a difference to the people around you. And you can't force performance only through hard work and dedication. There are other factors at play.

I've learned trauma is relative. The moment we start comparing trauma is the moment we should be looking inward. We all experience emotional wounding in our lives.

WHY I WROTE THIS BOOK

This book has been a labor of love and is a profound shift from my first book published in 2017. Here's why:

Back then, I felt like a hard-headed, ex-corporate leader and determined scholar. I was on a mission to prove a point. With every draft of my first book, my intention only grew tougher. This time, with each corner I've turned, my intention has become softer, as I've realized more and more how interconnected our work and personal life is. I had always kept them so compartmentalized, out of what felt like necessity. I knew cognitively that they weren't separate, but my writing this book has been a deeply felt emotional realization that nothing in life is separate. Everything is connected.

I started this book as a personal memoir. It was going to be called *The Perfect Widow*. The grips of perfectionism not even loosening in the role of a widow. But so much of my identity, like most of us, was tied up in work, and much of my trauma was playing out in my professional life. Grief and sadness are in the workplace too—because they're in our lives.

What I've learned is that writing is less about making a point and more about asking the right questions. It's about gently exploring potential, opportunity, and unknowns, and inviting you, reading this, into the conversation. I'm not right. Nobody is wrong. These are things that are simply important for us to explore. Concepts that must evolve as our understanding of why and how things work evolve too. Writing is a way to open doors, not barge through them. It's a delicate process, and it's one to be treated with grace and compassion.

When this book was nothing but an idea, it wasn't actually even a book, as such. It was going to be a love letter to my sons, a memoir about a hard but very beautiful life and journey we have been on together. The teen years were drawing to a close, and with each day I would see another image of what adulthood might look like for them. Nothing ages you more than reflecting on how quickly your children turn from babies, to teens, to young adults.

I spent months pouring thoughts and feelings onto paper and into audio. Many of these things had been living deep within me, never so much as hinting that they might come that close to the surface. After months and months, 60,000 words found their way outward, with an explicit intention to release my boys from my story, so they could leave their teenage years and enter adulthood unencumbered by my shadows, my stories, and my imperfections but also with some wisdom on how to navigate suffering that will invariably show up in their futures.

I was so wrapped up in my emotions that I had missed an obvious connection. Thankfully, my wise coach Leisse Wilcox gently pointed out that my writing could be serving a broader audience and how it was, in fact, very aligned to my professional work.

That was the catalyst for this book and the Evolved Leadership Model. My story was simply the case study demonstrating that three principles—self-awareness, self-regulation, co-regulation—open the door to higher levels of leadership. I was proof that self-awareness is impossible when you're out of balance.

The concepts and ideas that I discuss in this book are grounded in neuroscience and psychology research to help explain the "why" of certain things. However, I can assure you there won't be extensive medical explanations or complex psychoanalysis.

WE CAN ALL MAKE A DIFFERENCE

If you're committed to building a healthy workplace culture that is grounded in human leadership, then I believe that makes you a leader. It's people like you who create change. Please amplify your voice and make a difference where you can. Of course, if you have direct reports or even an entire division or company that look to you as their leader, you will benefit from reading this book.

You're the people I envisioned as I wrote these chapters.

As you read this book, I invite you to think of yourself: look inward and get curious. I've ended each chapter with reflection questions to help you. They are based on my Evolved Leadership Principles, and I welcome you to put them into action by:

- observing a behavioral pattern
- being conscious of your emotions and using them as data points
- being curious in how you connect with others, contemplating if it leads them to feel safe or protective

That's the key to unlocking performance in your teams: looking more deeply at yourself. Your expanded self-awareness removes unconscious barriers limiting the connection and safety others feel with you.

Evolve isn't only the evolution of leadership. It's the evolution of what being a leader even means. It's an evolution of what we believe. To lead isn't to direct, to tell, or even to teach. To lead is to go first. It is to become so deeply self-aware, so obviously flawed but accepting of who we really are that we give everyone around us permission to be who they are too. And in doing so, we create safe cultures and environments for people to flourish.

I know the topic of trauma may feel intense and elicit strong reactions, so please pay attention to your needs. My goal is to discuss what it means to be trauma-informed as a leader, not to ask anyone to examine their own trauma or analyze it for others. If you're noticing extreme discomfort or strong reactions, please put down the book and reach out to a health-care provider.

Finally, this book is not about advice, it's an invitation to consider a new perspective. It's about real people who are living their lives and doing their best but aren't aware that unhealed trauma, unconscious behaviors, and adaptive patterns are impacting their reactions and day-to-day life. It's taking them to places they don't want to be in or don't have the words to describe what's happening. We can't avoid experiencing some sort of trauma, so it's time to get real about it.

You might feel lost and hopeless at work right now. I see you and want you to know you're not alone.

Let's take a walk down a new path of conversation and understand how trauma informs our leadership by influencing how much permission we give others to be honest, vulnerable, and brave in their pursuit of being wholly and completely themselves.

I'm glad you're here. Let's do this together.

CHAPTER 1

WORK IS IN CRISIS

Lengthy commutes have been part of my working life for as long as I can remember—driving to and from the office, skillfully navigating through traffic and weather conditions for close to two hours each day. Spending that amount of time locked in a car might be a nightmare for some, but I've always enjoyed it. There's no one but me and my music.

One bright sunny June day in 2003, I was cruising down Hwy 400 just outside of Toronto, Whitesnake blaring through my car speakers. I put my hand on my belly and could feel the kicks of my unborn child. I wondered whether he was telling me to turn it down or that he loved my taste in '80s' music. I smiled while thinking of our future together.

I pulled into the parking lot at work, turned off the music, and took a deep breath to prepare for the walk inside. With only a few short weeks until our son was born, each day was getting physically harder. The pause before getting out of the car also allowed me to pull myself together and put on my game face. This made it easier for everyone, and I didn't want people to feel awkward. What do you say to a pregnant woman whose husband has received a stage 4 cancer diagnosis?

This was my reality for the last few months before our first son was born. I was trying hard to stay positive and optimistic. At work, I continued performing to my high standards and tried not to let myself get lost in what-ifs, but if I was honest, the truth was always lurking deep within me. I just didn't know how to face it, and work was a great distraction. I was young and ambitious and had an amazing manager who had taken me under her wing. Learning alongside her was exciting, so that's where I tried to focus.

After the birth of our son, my parental leave was brief. I took only four months, and it was starkly different from what other parents I knew experienced. Much of that time was spent supporting Paul during his immunotherapy, which occurred out of the country in Pittsburgh. Visiting Daddy in the hospital and going for walks in unfamiliar neighborhoods near the hospital aren't typical activities in the first few months for a new mom and her newborn.

Shortly after my return to work, I was confronted by a seemingly innocent question: "Didn't you just have a baby?" It felt like an invitation to be a proud mom, so I reached for a picture to show my cute son. Then the real question dropped, and I put the photo away: "Why are you back so soon?" In Canada, we have a generous parental leave program that gives parents up to a year off after the arrival of a child.

I had only taken four months. Shame enveloped me in an instant, and I quickly snapped, "Well, you'd be back to work this quickly too if your husband was dying." The disconnection and isolation I felt was intense. I desperately wanted to disappear.

That aggressive type of outburst never happened again. It was safer to keep my feelings hidden at work, so I buried them as I walked the halls of a big, bustling corporation. By the time our second son was born eighteen months later, I had become an expert in keeping my worlds separate. All around me people were hustling—busy trying to reach targets, creating innovative products, and staying connected and dedicated to doing their work. Everyone looked so normal. No one knew how lonely and sad I was feeling.

I was in a crisis. My life was in chaos, it was changing fast, and I was desperate to find a new normal under our extenuating circumstances. I did my best to enjoy moments, but I was feeling lost and even hopeless at times. Disconnection and isolation felt like the safest options I had.

My leaders and colleagues were incredible supporters and I'm truly grateful for how accommodating they were. It was a priceless gift during such difficult times. There were a few other individuals grappling with similar adversity in our big company, and there was more than enough support to go around. I was lucky Paul's illness hadn't happened in 2020 when the crisis of the pandemic shattered everyone's world and ruined our support systems.

PANDEMIC SEISMIC SHIFTS

We are humans who happen to be workers, not workers who happen to be human.

Efficient performance doesn't happen by selecting the "work harder" button or pushing through because you're tough, strong, and motivated. Humanity is so much more than *doing*.

Doing makes us feel accomplished, and we often get rewarded with praise and promotions. There just isn't enough time to slow down the pace. On March 11, 2020, when the World Health Organization declared COVID-19 a pandemic, we were suddenly forced to stop, whether we wanted to or not.

I think back to the hustle before 2020: getting kids to school, racing into the office to log endless hours of work in person, then speeding back home to feed the family and drive the kids to some sort of activity in an arena, auditorium, or studio. Every time I think about that era, it brings on a deep exhale. I feel the weight of it because the reality is we have rarely treated ourselves and the people we work with as humans first, letting aspirations for efficiency and productivity take priority. This has been the cornerstone of corporate success, and as dutiful employees, we've fallen into step.

A seismic shift has happened.

The unknown of the pandemic was terrifying. The isolation was painful. The hibernation lasted far longer than anyone thought it would, and now, as office workers reorganize back into collective spaces, we see traditional norms and expectations being challenged.

"Why do I have to work every day in an office?" "What does business attire mean now?"

We had to change overnight how we worked. All the beliefs and resistance to "remote working" were shoved aside because we had to find a way—there was no other choice. The lockdowns continued for longer than expected, so people adapted. Those with the greatest amount of privilege, like those who work in offices, learned that they could do their job remotely. The pandemic has completely challenged and uprooted beliefs about productivity at work. We can't go back to the old way because there is proof that we can work differently, but what that new balance is between employee and employer isn't yet clear. It's not the old way, and it's not 100 percent remote. There is a happy medium, but to find it, we have to give time and space to heal.

Here's the big question: Will leadership really be any different than it was pre-pandemic?

It's too soon to know for sure, but the pressure continues to mount as employee burnout rates soar to new highs.[1] Many organizations espouse the importance of employee health and wellness, especially with the pandemic's illumination on the topic. But the fact remains that programs and policies aren't able to keep pace with demands.

While employers work to create healthier systems, leaders as key influencers in the system have the best opportunity to instill real change; however, they will need to turn inward and truly examine themselves. In *American Detox*, author Kerri Kelly notes, "[o]ur refusal to face the truth of our collective traumas dooms us to perpetually reenact them."[2]

We work in an organizational ecosystem that is complex and interconnected with unpredictable events unfolding almost every day. In North America, we're juggling country-wide internet outages, overburdened hospitals, airports, and emergency systems, and high levels of inflation—all these factors are creating chaos and high levels of stress. This depletes us when it happens day after day and we don't have the tools to manage our mental health and emotional well-being. When we don't have the tools to understand the conscious and unconscious behaviors and emotions we're seeing in ourselves and our teams, we can't replace unproductive behaviors with new ones.

We can feel lost, hopeless, and depleted.

In Workhuman's *State of Human Connection at Work Spring 2022 Report* that analyzed the work experience of more than 2,000 employees in the United States, Canada, and parts of the UK, 58 percent of employees say they're working on autopilot, and 44 percent report they're having trouble concentrating on work.[3] The paper notes that distinct lines are being drawn between the experience of "2D versus 3D" employees, depending on whether they work mostly remotely or spend at least some of their time working directly with people and materials.

Now leaders need to be effective in person and virtually. It's become more complicated.

We've gone through the pandemic together, but the experience has been unique for each of us depending on our level in the organization, type of work, demographics, and degree of privilege, to name a few factors. What we may not all realize is that we've all had trauma and we now have an opportunity to name it and address it.

As neuroscientist David Rock notes, we felt this collective trauma from three sources—the lack of certainty about what would happen next, the level of confusion and overwhelm as a result of the lack of control over our situation, and the profound loneliness we felt in prolonged times of isolation.[4] We might not have felt these to the same degree or in the same ways, but combined, they became a prolonged, shared traumatic event. We won't recover in weeks or months. It will take years.

THERE'S NO BUFFER LEFT AND FEAR IS TAKING OVER

For years, companies have focused on serving clients and shareholders. They create value through innovative products and services, and this generates a profit for shareholders. Looking after their employees has not been their first priority.

In this model, the belief is that when we serve the customer, it will create loyalty and, in return, more sales. It would be too capitalistic to say we work only to please our shareholders, so it's disguised by statements putting customers first.

It has now become obvious that we have served our customers and our clients on the backs of our employees and there's not much left to give. There's no buffer. We have maximized our efficiency and productivity in service of the client.

Even a massive global event that shut down offices wasn't going to stop the machine of capitalism. We slowed down for a brief time, but it wasn't realistic to think that performance objectives would be drastically reduced. As Tara Haelle notes, we had been relying on "surge capacity" to get through the initial phases of the pandemic, a term defined by psychologist and professor Ann Masten, that Haelle explains as "a collection of adaptive systems—mental and physical—that humans draw on for short-term survival in acutely stressful situations, such as natural disasters."[5] It was the rush of getting things done as best we could at the start, thinking it wouldn't last long. But as time wore on, the surge became an energy depletion, and we had no way to recharge it even though performance expectations somehow stayed the same or even grew.

Do you really want this continual push for performance and overworking to exist for the next generation? Are we going to consider the last three years as a series of events and overlook the trauma and emotional turmoil it has inflicted on us? I look at my sons who, in their late teens, are already in the workforce, and I see the gap in how people are treated. Compassion is low on the list.

It's hard to be compassionate when you're trying to navigate so much uncertainty and still generate predictable profits. The embedded beliefs of profits first are hard to change, and until now the emotional aspect of the workplace could be pushed aside. It's a hierarchical "power over others" self-sustaining system, where power is recognized, understood and shared between a small group of individuals. It brings predictability and control but at the expense of too many people.

Companies getting called out for treating employees poorly isn't new. Yet we continue to hear stories about leaders making decisions that don't benefit employees and about leaders who demand their team work through extreme conditions. There still exist leaders who install productivity software in their company to monitor performance without informing their people because they don't realize their impact and they are trying to get results in a logical way.

Evolving our leadership allows people to be humans at work. It brings the full scope of human behavior into the workplace, and not only logic, but instincts and emotions as well. This makes leadership even harder because dealing with emotions and instincts will always have a degree of unpredictability and uncertainty.

Then layer on global events like the pandemic, social injustice, wars, and famines. Uncertainty surrounds us and our brains desperately struggle to keep up. Fear sets in and we cannot be vulnerable.

According to renowned researcher Brené Brown, vulnerability is the emotion we experience when there is uncertainty, risk, and emotional exposure.[6] Telling your boss you think they're wrong—that's risky. Asking to work from home because you can be more productive—that feels risky too. Sharing your perspective in a team meeting when your background and experience is vastly different—that's incredibly risky. Who knows how people will react? It's easier to stay quiet. And the more this happens, the more disconnected we feel.

We need predictability at work because our performance is being evaluated on a regular basis and that's linked to our compensation. Predictability equals safety and being safe at work gives us the security that we can keep the roof over our heads and food on the table.

When the uncertainty lasts, fear settles in more deeply. It influences our behavior in conscious and unconscious ways. We might stay quiet on an issue or not even realize we've stopped trying. As Kelly notes in *American Detox*, "But when fear isn't realized or resolved, it gets imprinted in the body and normalized, shaping our beliefs and behaviors, and even our bodies. And with overexposure to triggering images in culture and media, we become predisposed to fear. Fear plays tricks with our minds, altering our perception of reality. It impacts our bodies, short-circuiting our rational response pathways, creating levels of stress, and manifesting as disease and dis-ease. We learn to live with our fear—even collude with it. To cope, we avoid, we numb, we get busy, we seek to control everything. Before we know it, fear becomes how we move in the world."[7]

WHY EVERY LEADER NEEDS TO BE TRAUMA-INFORMED

You're likely burned out from juggling your own life and work priorities through the pandemic, followed by helping both your family members and your team do the same. Deloitte's 2021 report analyzing the well-being of senior leaders globally indicated more than eight in ten senior leaders (82 percent) experienced exhaustion indicative of burnout risk. Ninety-six percent of those who reported exhaustion indicate that their mental health has declined.[8] Further, the report highlights that the pandemic has created increased stress for leaders given the increased complexity, decreased control, and reduced staff support, all contributing to burnout risk.

And then there's the massive issue of managing workload. The National Standard for Canada for Psychological Health and Safety in the Workplace includes workload management as a major factor for burnout.[9] We are far beyond the "productivity conversations" and yet, because of the reduced number of employees, leaders are still looking for ways to be more productive instead of addressing the unrealistic workload volumes.

We need to break the destructive cycle of overworking and valuing performance at all costs. The lifetime costs of toxic stress, adversity, and trauma are estimated by the CDC to be over $120 billion.[10] This is a business issue that needs attention and trauma-informed leadership is part of the solution. We need to expect employees to upload boundaries that align with their contracted work arrangements, not push them to work longer hours to "prove" their commitment.

Your ability to look at your own work performance with fresh eyes is part of this evolution. Your ongoing self-awareness and efforts to step out of this cycle will be part of the new shift that's needed.

These are incredibly challenging workplace conditions for us to survive in, let alone thrive. We need to pause and take stock of the trauma that surrounds us. As the Crisis & Trauma Resources Institute (CTRI) notes, trauma-informed leadership "moves beyond relational leadership in that trauma-informed leaders understand and are aware of the impact of trauma in the workplace. And they want to be part of the solution to supporting those affected by trauma."[11]

This doesn't mean you need to become an expert in trauma or be able to diagnose trauma in yourself or others. All that's needed from you is the understanding that the people on your team and others you encounter throughout your day, including family members, customers, and everyone else in your community, have all experienced trauma to varying degrees. As we'll talk about in Chapters 8 and 9, your job is to focus on managing your own responses. And I'll show you how to do that.

If you're reading this and thinking, *great, I'm already self-aware so I don't need to read any further*, not so fast. I thought the same thing too, and I was adamant I was one of the better ones. That was my ego talking, and I fell into her trap. The type of self-awareness we need for leaders today is an ongoing process and we need more leaders to step into it. In the next chapter, we'll talk about the ideal environment to support this type of leadership growth.

REFLECTIONS ON YOUR EVOLVED LEADERSHIP JOURNEY

1. How did the pandemic impact your work?

2. How does allowing people to be more "human" impact productivity?

3. What was your initial reaction to the term "trauma-informed leadership"?

CHAPTER 2

EVOLVING THE LEADERSHIP PATH

The year 2022 was a milestone one in which I turned fifty. I planned multiple celebrations with friends and family throughout the year. I had so much to be grateful for, and it couldn't be packed all into one day. One of my favorite events was planned by my husband and landed a few days before my actual birthday. It was a fine-dining experience at Alo, one of Toronto's most prestigious restaurants.

We enjoyed a seven-course meal filled with unique tastes and delicious flavors that delighted our palettes. We had the best seats in the house: a rounded corner booth that gave us a view of the entire restaurant—the chefs in the kitchen, the servers, and the sommelier. From this vantage point, we could admire how the staff flowed together in unison as if they were dancing.

I glanced toward the floor, curious about how the women could glide so smoothly wearing heels in this seemingly choreographed routine. When I caught the moving feet of our server, I did a double take. Were those running shoes? No way, not in one of Canada's finest restaurants! It had to be a mistake, an anomaly for this one person. I looked around at everyone's feet. I was shocked. They were all wearing running shoes.

Puzzled, we asked our server about it. Her response was simple. After months of being closed due to the pandemic, they could no longer tolerate the fancy dress shoes and heels while being on their feet for so many hours. Running shoes were much more comfortable. They decided unanimously they couldn't go back to such constricted footwear.

Even more surprising was that there wasn't a set standard. The shoes all varied in color and design. But when I looked closer, I could see the brand was the same. They were all New Balance.

I leaned back into my seat and smiled at the symbolism of those shoes. Here I was, celebrating a new decade of life and discovering my own "new balance," while at the same time helping leaders navigate what a "new balance" would look like in their offices.

A NEW STYLE OF LEADERSHIP IS POSSIBLE

People are doing the best they can. Do you believe this? I know not everyone does. However, in all my years of coaching and leading, I've never met someone who wakes up each day thinking, *I'm going to be a real jackass at work today.*

I believe leaders are doing the best they can with the tools they have. They shoulder a great deal of responsibility between meeting company objectives and holding direct reports accountable for their performance. It's not easy.

Your own experience with leaders is likely quite varied, ranging from amazing to abhorrent. Unfortunately, leaders don't all use the same toolbox, nor can they all use the tools they're given in the same way. We have different experiences, beliefs, and abilities. When the pandemic happened, the chaos and uncertainty threw many leaders into unknown territory, and for many, their toolkit didn't seem adequate enough to handle the reality of what they were facing.

Let me share an example of what this looks like for my teenage sons who work in the food service industry. We'll start with Manager A who is calm and unflustered, even when fryer oil burns an employee's foot and they have to go to the hospital (yes, that was my kid). When faced with requests for shift changes, Manager A handles them with a clear set of decision criteria understood by everyone; sometimes it works out, and sometimes the change can't be accommodated.

Manager B is a very different type of leader. Every question or request for clarification is met with derision or scorn; orders are barked out, leaving people feeling undervalued and disrespected. Requests for schedule changes to this manager are often declined without any consideration or attempt to accommodate them. In fact, it's as if the employees are widgets in a machine who need to conform to the leader's whim, the same way every time, with no room for variability.

Two managers, working in an identical work environment, with two very different styles. Manager A receives accolades from staff and management alike, both for how they manage the day-to-day operations as well as other variables including order processing times and customer satisfaction.

I have no doubt that Manager B is doing the best they can. They are trying to get performance in a fast-paced environment and perhaps think that they need to behave a certain way at work. Leadership expectations can be written but are sometimes passed along quietly or even by observation or osmosis. It's just "the way things are done here."

What's similar between Manager A and B is that they are both trying to inspire good performance from employees so that company objectives set by senior executives are consistently met. This is the case across many industries and organizations.

It's a tricky balance for leaders, especially after the pandemic. How do they hold employees accountable for performance while being flexible and recognizing the humanity of their employees who also happen to be parents, caregivers, and partners?

I have no doubt that you can relate. I don't need to know anything about your role or where you are to know that this is likely true. We are all on the receiving end of a wide range of leadership competencies, with some feeling more human-centered than others.

The fact remains that we get paid to deliver outcomes, so we do require performance expectations to stay aligned. We can't expect leaders to cater completely to our personal needs, but we can expect to be treated with respect, kindness, and transparency, all of which are elements of "human leadership."

Research from Gartner in 2022 points clearly to the need for "human leadership," but only 29 percent of employees believe their manager meets this standard.1 It's hard to embody these values when there's so much uncertainty and unpredictability in our business environments.

So what then does human leadership really mean? The Gartner article describes Human Leadership as having three components: authenticity, empathy, and adaptability. Circling back to Managers A and B, we can see a distinct difference in their empathy skills and ability to adapt to changing circumstances. And who was more authentic? That's right, Manager A.

Authenticity is not something you can teach or a tool you can put in a box. It's something you discover through experience and increased self-awareness and being mindful of your reactions and your impact. We'll talk more about authenticity in Chapter 8, but for now it's important to know that it's incredibly difficult to be authentic when fear is present.

In 2020, fear embraced us all when our physical safety was threatened by a global virus. Our foundational need for safety, at the base of Maslow's hierarchy of needs, was at risk. As the pandemic wore on, many leaders and employees were pushed beyond their limits, as safety and security continued to be compromised. When our survival instinct is at the forefront, fear underpins our behavior, and there is little room for compassion and patience.

In the countless conversations I had with people at all levels in organizations, they admitted to being beyond stressed and feeling unrecognized, undervalued, and unappreciated. There were real-life stories like the parent working from home and trying to take a call with their boss after 5 p.m. because that's the only time that would fit in the schedule, and they are embarrassed that their three-year-old is screaming in the background. Or the nurse at the vaccination clinic telling me the hospital administration only thinks of itself and doesn't have a clue what's really happening on the front lines. Then there are the employees who recounted how their managers continued to displace their anger and frustration onto the team, thus creating an authoritative dynamic with little room for discussion.

It's safe to say that our tanks are depleted and we're running on empty. Feelings that have been ignored, pushed down, or overlooked have nowhere to hide. Our energy has leaked out at a furious pace, and there's no time to recharge. People are exhausted and resigned to the fact that nothing will change. Yet we push through and hope our performance can keep up.

I've been there, believing I could think my way to sustained work performance. I could push that one little bit further to make it to the next day. Then one day turns into a week, which turns into a month, which turns into years. Feelings muted, my spirit dampened, I simply tolerated the people around me and lost all passion. This is what burnout looked like for me. I'm guessing you've been there too or are precariously close.

Although we have faced major workplace transformations and

corporate upheavals, the pandemic pushed us faster and harder than any previous change initiative. It dramatically changed how we look at work across demographic and generational lines, leaving us rethinking all aspects of how we work. We can't simply tell managers to lead better. We need to clarify what skills are needed to lead well in this next era of work.

We need to be the kind of leaders who are going to care for others *and* ourselves as we lead through the uncertainty and changing workplace needs, and this means navigating ambiguity and uncertainty without letting fear guide our behavior.

If we want productive employees who are accountable and innovative, then we need to focus on creating the optimal conditions to make this happen. People need team dynamics that value calmness over anxiety and leaders who manage their emotions well. This leads to psychological **safety**, and when this is done with **consistency**, people's stress responses will be lowered, which in turn lowers fear and invites **authenticity**. It is in these types of spaces that empathy can flourish, trust grows, and teams can adapt quickly to changing conditions.

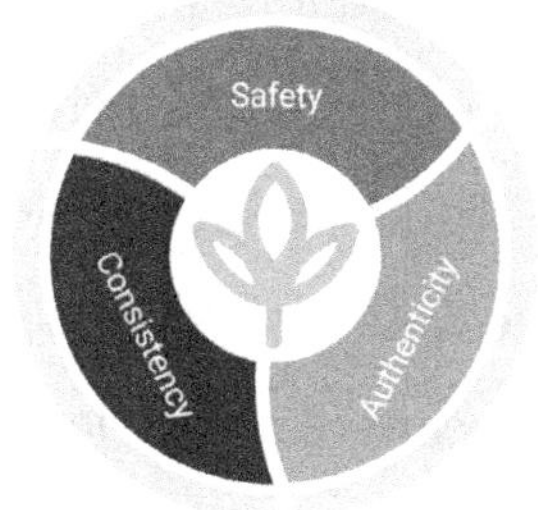

Think of a great leader you've worked with and I'll bet these elements of safety, consistency, and authenticity were present in your interactions with them. I recall a time with one of my best leaders when I was faced with a challenging situation. Our team had identified information that posed a significant reputational risk to the organization. My manager had shown a consistent calm demeanor in our few months working together, so I trusted she wouldn't panic or cast blame. I approached her with the situation. Within a few hours, we hypothesized various solutions, some of which were quite unorthodox, and came up with a resolution. The risk was averted in a timely manner.

The combination of safety, consistency, and authenticity is paramount for teams. Think of all the issues that are buried or avoided when these conditions don't exist.

THE WIDENING GAP BETWEEN MANAGERS AND EMPLOYEES

The performance expectations for office-based workers may have subsided for a brief time when the pandemic started, but it didn't take long before productivity rebounded back as a top priority for leaders.

In 2022, as we were adapting to pandemic life, a survey from Deloitte and Workplace Intelligence showed that while more than 80 percent of senior leaders in organizations in four countries felt their employees were "thriving in all aspects of their well-being," employees ranked their well-being significantly lower across four categories including physical, mental, social, and financial.[2] It's not shocking that senior leaders aren't in tune with the sentiments and situations of their employees, and it's proof that we need more evolved leaders.

From the 1950s through to the late 1980s, working more than a standard eight-hour day was something to be celebrated. Companies promised lifetime employment, receiving lifetime loyalty from their employees in return, so the idea of "work-to-rule" was seen as a selfish act. I remember retirement parties early in my career in the late '90s. I admired the dedication of those people who had served their organization for twenty-five, thirty, and sometimes even forty years. Loyalty appeared to be valued and admired.

But let's remember that the relationship between employee and employer is a contractual one. Both parties sign an employment agreement and commit to upholding it. I don't know of any other contract where it is expected that you deliver beyond the set terms. Sure, there are performance-based bonuses in some roles, but those conditions are clearly laid out (like when profit targets are exceeded).

So how did the expectation of doing more at work for the same pay become normalized? Because there was another unwritten contract at play.

In my first book, *Rules of Engagement*, I talked about the social contract between employees and employers—the unwritten expectations they have—and how it was shifting. There was a growing trend of employees feeling less motivated by loyalty and hard work and demanding more balance in their lives. The pandemic threw this social contract forward exponentially. Employers suddenly found themselves unable to mandate or force people back into offices.

It's not much wonder then that the term "quiet quitting" went viral in 2022, a reference to employees choosing to only do the minimum requirements of their job.

Some leaders claimed the term was too negative and that we

shouldn't be using it. Other leaders emphasized that in times of limited staffing, inflation, and a possible recession, this was the time for "stepping up and doing whatever needs to be done." A *Forbes* article by Bryan Robinson PhD pointed out that 98 percent of managers of "quiet quitters" said it's important their reports do more than the bare minimum.[3]

There is no single right solution for quiet quitting, but one thing is clear: the hustle culture that was once revered and garnered employee loyalty is being seriously challenged.

Large corporations like Apple, Goldman Sachs, and Netflix tried to mandate workers back into the office despite pushback from employees (and even petitions from some).[4] Apple changed their stance a few times, indicating a true power struggle. Working from home during the pandemic was proof that we could be productive outside of the office. Leaders forcing employees back into the office won't erase this fact. If we can get work done from home, then why can't we find a balance that meets the needs of employers and employees? Because for many, trust comes only when I can "see" what you're doing. That's the problem with unwritten contracts.

The employer is asking more than their employees are contractually required to provide because they've been able to in the past, but the tables are turning and concepts like quiet quitting spread quickly because they're resonating deeply with people.

So what are we really quitting? It's not the job or the people. It's the unwritten expectations and the imbalance of fairness that have benefited organizations to make more money on the backs of their employees in the name of loyalty. We are quitting old ways of working, unwritten expectations, and a system that has financially benefited a small few—the 1 percent at the top.

Who is asking people to come back to the office, mandating their physical presence at a desk? It is usually the ones who have the largest salaries, the most lavish offices, and the utmost safety of power by their position. They are also the ones most accountable to shareholders, so they are trying to keep both parties happy. But the collective employee group knows differently, and there is new momentum for change across countries, industries, and people.

WHERE DO WE GO FROM HERE?

Here's how I describe leadership through the pandemic: a power struggle between head and heart. The rational, analytic, and logical skills required to deliver performance seemed at odds with being empathic and understanding—important relational elements to inspire people.

What if I told you we've been overlooking a critical aspect of leadership, a third element to balance with head and heart?

We have three distinct centers of intelligence that can be leveraged in life and in leadership. You already know about the head and heart, but what about the body? Your nervous system gathers an incredible amount of data through the five senses, and it has been widely overlooked as a leadership tool.

The body as a center of intelligence might feel a little odd. We encourage people to go with their gut, yet we discourage decisions that aren't based on facts or data. The body is full of wisdom, however. As we'll discuss, it also carries trauma that disconnects you from this wisdom. Learning about trauma-informed leadership is one step closer to understanding how our body gives us this knowledge.

REFLECTIONS ON YOUR EVOLVED LEADERSHIP JOURNEY

1. What are your beliefs about quiet quitting and how might your current role influence that perspective?

2. How compelled are you to deliver beyond what is expected of you at work? What beliefs might be fueling that behavior?

3. When has fear been present for you in the past year at work? What does fear feel like in your body and where is it located?

CHAPTER 3

THREE CENTERS OF INTELLIGENCE

In 2013, I found myself unexpectedly in a senior leadership role as a director in a large pharmaceutical organization. It was in an area in which I had no technical experience. I felt exhilarated but, at the same time, scared and worried. Why did they think I could do this job? What did they see in me? It was my ability to build strong relationships, learn quickly, and inspire performance. I grounded myself in that and my fourteen years of experience in the company.

On the home front, there was another unexpected and welcomed surprise. His name was Don. After such sadness and grief, I was resolute about never again risking the possibility of that type of pain. But love showed up when I wasn't expecting it, enveloped me, and I sunk into the vulnerability of it once more.

It was a new life balanced with love and work.

We were only two months away from our wedding when I was asked to take on a new project in my director role. The decision to say no was not easy, but I didn't want to be consumed with work every night. I had been given a second chance at building a family with a partner, and I didn't want anything to interfere with that.

I respectfully declined the project and emphasized my desire to focus on the tasks I'd been assigned in the role. They were challenging enough, and I was still in learning mode. It was a pivotal moment in my career. I made a conscious choice that served my best interests instead of saying yes to please the executive team. I don't regret it for a second. However, the following few years were the most difficult in my professional life. My confidence, which had never been an issue, plummeted to an all-time low. I felt different than my colleagues, an outsider who didn't fit in anymore. I stayed quiet, and my usual thirst to learn dried up. I avoided challenging conversations and second-guessed my decisions.

At my core, I was afraid. Fear was guiding my behavior, but I didn't know it—it was an unconscious drive. I feared not being smart enough, of not having enough experience. Although I couldn't put it into words at that time, I know now that's what it was.

When we're in fear, we are trying to protect ourselves, and our ability to adapt to changing conditions is compromised. I was trying to protect my reputation as a great leader who was supportive of the corporate vision and strategy. I wanted to show that I was completely on board and "bought in" and that I could lead my team through transformational change. But I also wanted that new balance I had been gifted.

I loved being married to Don, but life at home was getting harder. We were trying to blend a family while I was juggling everything at work, and I foolishly thought that I had to do it all on my own. It had been five years since the boys had lost their father. Trying to squeeze all the joy of a lifetime into a few years before he passed had been my priority. Now I was afraid of failing as a mother—of not giving the boys the opportunity to feel joy and happiness because their childhood involved deep suffering.

I was determined not to succumb to the vulnerability of my emotions. I was strong and wouldn't crumble—there were too many people who needed me. It was a vicious cycle of performance and pleasing at all costs, both at home and at work. Even though no one was telling me out loud to do this, the world I grew up in screamed it in my ear. I didn't know how to turn down that volume let alone find the door that would let me out and show me other ways to be.

I started to notice differences in my body. There were more aches and pains, mystery changes, and weight gain. One day my back muscles seized so badly that I couldn't get out of bed. I had no idea what caused it, and I had to miss work for a few days. I was incredibly embarrassed because I couldn't point to a cause. All around me colleagues spoke of yoga, working out, running, cycling, and CrossFit. None of those things were part of my life. My athletic days had evaporated in my late twenties. Yet again I felt like an outsider and that I didn't belong.

My seized back was a warning sign from my body that the stress was getting to be too much. It's not much wonder given all that was unfolding around me. I felt like an island at work, believing in myself deep down but questioning so many things because I felt so out of place. At home, we were facing the challenges of teenagers with the emotional pain of grief and loss, all while trying to build a new, cohesive family unit. It was so much harder than I thought it would be. Everything around me felt so grueling. And as usual, my inner dialogue told me to push through. I told myself I had been through worse, so this was nothing in comparison.

About a year later, my role was made redundant. My corporate days came to a close with a generous package. For the first time in more than twenty years, I didn't have to be in an office or leading meetings or managing performance of direct reports. It was a strange feeling but apparently one that suited me, as my son declared a few days after my corporate dismissal, "You're so happy now, why didn't you leave work sooner?"

Good question. I thought a lot about it every day for months as I walked for hours through my neighborhood. For the first time in years, I was moving my body on a regular basis. I even hired a trainer and was in the gym three times a week. I was finally giving my body the attention it needed.

I had a bad habit of ignoring signs from my body indicating it was too stressed. I'll never know for certain, but I believe I was close to burnout for a second time. Being packaged out was a blessing in disguise because I was forced to find a new routine. Thankfully, I chose the path to reconnect with my body and was fortunate enough to have the space and time to commit to lasting changes.

Can you relate to this experience of working until your body literally collapses? I believe this reality is at crisis levels in our workplaces. People are depleted, trying to exist beyond their capacity but unable to find the physical energy or the emotional bandwidth to get through a day without crying, screaming, or numbing out.

Understandably, people can't leave the security provided by a regular salary, so they push through in a disconnected state. This translates to fewer conversations with colleagues and instead choosing short, terse emails; saying yes on the outside but no on the inside; snapping at loved ones because they are emotionally drained. If you're a manager, you're likely to find that top performers are not as reliable as they used to be, and more people are likely taking medical leaves than ever before. We're trying to push through it because that's what we've always done, yet our bodies are screaming no.

We push through out of ignorance, not realizing the body has so much wisdom and intelligence. It's rarely been part of our leadership training. If only we could listen better.

A concept slowly moving into mainstream leadership philosophies is that we are three-brained beings that function through three different centers of intelligence. These centers represent the three modes of perception, processing, and expression, with each center's function having its advantages and its disadvantages—its positive uses and its misuses, or ways it helps us interpret and interact with the world around us and ways it can steer us off course.[1]

The centers exist in all of us as the body center (sensations), the heart center (feeling), and the head center (thinking). When we can understand these different types of intelligence and access the right intelligence within us for the right task, new insight emerges and the ability to take better actions and make better choices become available to us.

In simple terms:

- The head center helps us observe, analyze, and understand complex things.
- The heart center helps us be emotionally connected, passionate, expressive, and in connection with others.
- The body center processes information from the five senses to take action and move things forward in an orderly and just manner.

All three centers of intelligence are accessible to us. When these centers are balanced, we can access them appropriately to successfully navigate through different situations life throws our way.

However, we are all born with a preference for one center. As a result, it can easily become our default and we end up using that center for every situation we face. This all happens on an unconscious level, but the good news is that you can become more conscious of your behavior by learning about the centers and your reactivity patterns.

Most of us are barely able to use one center effectively, let alone all three. Imagine the leadership potential that could be harnessed if we simply learned how to use our dominant center in an effective manner.

UNDERSTANDING OUR HEAD CENTER

When using the head center of intelligence, data and facts are the drivers of decisions. It looks for concrete facts, numbers, and evidence to support a plan or problem-solving solution. The head center likes to wait, explore alternatives, and embrace complexity. An option doesn't feel valid unless it's supported by objective data or appears to be unbiased, and ideas that sound like they are based on emotions or just by "gut" are discounted or ignored.

The head center of intelligence is important for helping us feel confident that our decisions are rational and will hold up to criticism from others. The risk is often the flip side of that same coin—facts are believed to be stronger evidence for an approach or decision, even if the facts aren't entirely aligned with the problem being solved.

Here's an example; perhaps it will sound familiar: You're in a meeting where all the division heads are expected to reduce their workforce by 10 percent because of missed revenue targets. You know it will cause a ripple effect in service delivery when certain roles are cut, and you know that the performance review data doesn't offer a complete picture of the capabilities within your team. Dave, for example, doesn't have strong communication skills (which are highly valued within your company), but he is an outstanding problem solver, even if his approach to analyzing a situation is unpopular with the rest of the team (his voice gets loud when he's deep into problem-solving mode). On paper, the data points to adding Dave to the layoff list, but you know that your team's performance is going to be significantly impacted as a result.

That's why "data" isn't always unbiased, but it's treated as if it is.

Business tends to favor the head center, and it's easy to see why. It's logical, predictable, and rational, which is exactly what we like when making important investments and financial decisions. We are encouraged to make decisions as leaders based on what the data is telling us, and we are reprimanded if we make choices based on emotions or our gut.

Those with a dominant head center of intelligence prefer to rely on data and facts to guide their actions—they find themselves seeking out additional information in order to feel comfortable with their choices and can struggle if more details can't be found.

UNDERSTANDING OUR HEART CENTER

The heart center is about connection and relationships. It relies on accessing the range of emotions you feel to help guide your choices and behavior. The heart center is passionate and energetic, and it thrives in subjectivity. When it's open, we are empathic, receptive to the needs of others, and tuned in to emotions.

Those with a dominant heart center of intelligence make emotional inputs the primary driver of actions and behaviors. They are able to listen deeply, and not necessarily to the words but to the tone and emotion. This can be seen as illogical by some and deeply compassionate and caring by others.

There are times in our roles as leaders when we feel compelled to make choices that reflect our emotions in the moment. I was faced with a situation like this as a sales manager when I felt an existing policy wasn't flexible enough. Our team had won a Top Performer's trip to the Caribbean. We had worked hard for twelve months and were overjoyed with the win, especially because we were the underdogs. Shortly after the announcement, the vice president reminded me that the sales associate who had joined our team two weeks after the cut-off date wouldn't be included, even though they had contributed to fifty weeks of effort. I was upset and wouldn't let it go. I couldn't believe that they could uphold this seemingly arbitrary rule. I was stuck in the heart center, and they were stuck in the head center. Instead of taking time to understand each other, we both dug in our heels, and it negatively impacted our working relationship.

At work in our roles as leaders, being seen as making emotional decisions can create problems for us. The challenge is finding the balance. Given the corporate preference for data, making choices based on emotions can be mocked or discounted if it's not balanced properly.

My dominant center of intelligence is the heart, and in looking back, I see how much I overused this center as a leader. My default reaction was always to protect and build relationships. Reactivity is unconscious and when we're stressed, it's much harder to control. Remember those years I was a director and often felt misunderstood?

I was completely imbalanced; I was stuck in the heart center, which made it difficult for people to see my strategic abilities.

UNDERSTANDING OUR BODY CENTER

Our body center of intelligence relies on accessing data from our senses as well as other somatic inputs (somatic comes from the word *soma*, meaning literally "of the body"). If you've ever been in a situation where you hear a startling noise and the hairs on the back of your neck stand up, you're relying on body intelligence.

Those who have a dominant body center experience inner sensations and have a good gut sense of things. This guides their actions, and they trust their instincts to do the right thing, but details may be difficult to explain to other people. When I'm hungry, I can't explain why I'm craving a burger—maybe my iron is low or perhaps I haven't had enough protein that day. I just know I really, really want to have a burger for lunch.

When the body center of intelligence is operating in a healthy manner, it is grounded and present. Reality is perceived through the five senses, and one can listen to the sensations in their body. They can act with conviction and feel empowered. However, when the body center is unhealthy, one's behavior is mindless, impulsive, and excessive.

How do you use the body as a center of intelligence at work? It guides us in answering the question, "What is my gut telling me to do?" You might evaluate a situation without an obvious path forward, looking at data and analysis, and you may also possibly consider the emotions at play. Without a clear answer, you may be left with choosing how to move forward based on instinct. You can work backward from there to validate that choice by using some of the data available or pointing to the emotional impact of other choices, but in the back of your mind, you know you're simply "going with your gut."

When this center is dominant, you take action quickly because it feels right. There is wisdom here based on past experiences, patterns, and somatic inputs. But we don't often talk about this in leadership. Why? I think it's because of the variability and the subjectivity. This center is very instinctual and can't be standardized. Like all the centers, it can be used in unhealthy ways as well.

Body intelligence can be rewarded if the choices are seen as smart ones, particularly if they reduce the decision-making time and work out favorably in the end. They might be challenged if gut decisions are viewed as reckless or unsupported.

What's important here is understanding that for many of us, using our body center of intelligence can offer new data points not previously considered. It adds a layer of instinct to consider that can lead to a more well-rounded or considered choice or set of actions and shouldn't be dismissed as unreliable.

ACCESSING THESE DIFFERENT TYPES OF INTELLIGENCE

As we look at how to better leverage the range of inputs available to us, it's helpful to consider first which center of intelligence we rely on most often to help us navigate situations and decisions.

It's not a simple answer, and there are many nuances. But here are a few questions to start you off. Think about a recent stressful or complex situation you needed to solve at work. Take yourself back to that moment and consider the sources of information available, what you needed to guide your decision, and if there was anything you discounted as you deliberated. As you think about how you made the final choice, was your instinct to:

- Find more information/data/resources to understand the full picture before deciding? Did you prefer the big picture first before getting into details?
  If yes, you might be a head-dominant type.

- Consider the emotions or feelings of the people impacted by your decision? Were you comfortable going with the flow and not needing things to make sense?
  If yes, you might be a heart-dominant type.

- Pause and see if your gut was pushing you to make a particular choice? Did you think best when you were moving or doing something?
  If yes, you might be a body-dominant type.

It's important to recognize that while you might have a dominant source of intelligence that feels like it's served you well, you might not be using it in a healthy way. Over-reliance on one particular center type will result in missed opportunities or poorer outcomes. The reality is that most of us rely on our dominant center of intelligence without even knowing it.

IT'S ALL ABOUT BALANCE

Most leaders operate from one dominant source of intelligence—the head (thinking types), heart (feeling types), or body (gut types). This isn't to say that you don't or can't use strengths from all three, but most of us draw from a primary source of intelligence.

When you learn about these centers, it evolves your self-awareness, and leadership can become less draining and much less reactive. That's because we gain more understanding and respect for other styles instead of flippantly reacting with "they're a jerk" or "they aren't on board" or "what a flake."

As authors Sharon K. Ball and Renée Siegel note in their book *Reclaiming You: Using the Enneagram to Move from Trauma to Resilience*, "[w]hen you operate in an integrated way, accessing your body, heart, and mind, your response to life events is more balanced. This allows your life to run more smoothly."[2]

To find more balance in your centers, consider these questions:

- If you're a head-dominant type, are there additional data points to consider based on emotions or senses? Can you pause and ask yourself, *What is my gut telling me?*
- If you're a heart-dominant type, are there facts you're ignoring or any gut instincts that are hard to pinpoint but might be important?

- And if you're a body-dominant type, what are you missing that listening to your head or your heart might highlight for you?

In every case, learning to pause and ask yourself what else might be important to consider as you draw conclusions or make decisions is important for today's leaders. It can expand the options for what may be possible, resulting in better outcomes. It's not an easy practice, but it's one that can become critical.

As the landscape of priorities for workers is changing following the pandemic, your employees are considering their own options from head, heart, and gut instincts about the type of life and lifestyle they want to have. Your ability to respect all three centers of intelligence will help you stay grounded and mindful in your responses.

Let's look at the earlier workforce reduction example from a place of balanced, integrated centers of intelligence.

- Conversations with senior leaders and human resources have provided input into the required number of layoffs that will keep productivity at the required levels and meet budget restrictions. A plan has been created and shared with leaders in advance of the day the layoffs will take place.
- An outplacement agency will support employees impacted by the layoffs the day of and for up to six months after. This same agency will run workshops a few weeks prior for managers to help them process how they might feel in the

moment and how their direct reports may feel physically and emotionally when receiving the news.

- On the day of the event, leaders hold a team meeting to advise them of the situation, welcome questions to ensure employees have the proper facts, and if needed, encourage people to take time for the rest of the day to get grounded and reset.

When all sources of intelligence are considered up front, people feel more supported and respected, even in an exceptionally difficult situation.

With practice, leaders can draw from all three centers of intelligence, broadening their ability to create solutions that align the facts, emotions, and instincts, thus optimizing the likelihood of success as a result.

I know how hard it is to work from a place where all three centers of intelligence are integrated equally in our work. We naturally have an affinity for one type, sometimes two, but rarely all three.

Here are some ways to add the benefits from other centers of intelligence based on where you naturally draw from today:

If you are a head-dominant type and default easily to facts:

- What emotions could be considered in the situation? (heart)
- What sensations or "gut feelings" are present, pulling you to reconsider the data in front of you? (body)

- Do you think about how long a feeling will take before it goes away? (if yes, this may indicate an overactive head center)

If you are a heart-dominant type and default easily to emotions or relationships:

- What facts or data points are you glossing over that might help things make more sense? (head)
- What is your body sensing that you might also want to consider? (body)
- Do you get reactive when asked to be more rational, almost defending against using the other centers? (if yes, this may indicate an overactive heart center)

If you are a body-dominant type and default easily to a gut instinct:

- What additional information should you pause to consider first? (head)
- How might this decision impact the relationship? What might people be feeling? (heart)
- Do you judge people for not acting fast enough? (if yes, this may indicate and overactive body center)

What's critical as you think about the different types is to consider what center of intelligence is the right one for the right task.

- Where do you need to focus on the facts in a situation? (head)

- Where does understanding the emotions that might be the motivating factor in a person's behavior help shine new insight into a situation? (heart)
- When you pause to listen to what your gut might be telling you to do before you act, what other options might be possible? (body)

For nearly thirty years, I have participated in multiple leadership programs, read hundreds of books, and consumed hours of podcasts and lectures. Leadership skills were most often divided into two areas—head and heart. The best leaders blended a balance of both to guide their decision-making and strategic thinking while building strong relationships and inspiring people.

A third area of intelligence—our body—impacts our behavior just as much as the head and heart centers. The body's nervous system gathers insight through our five senses, making it a leadership tool that is widely unrealized and underutilized.

When we can accept the body as an important source of intelligence, we have new data we can use. And if we can accept that it works synergistically with our heads and hearts, we are one step closer to new insights and better leadership.

But what happens if our body's nervous system is compromised and not functioning to its full potential? We'll learn about this in the next chapter.

REFLECTIONS ON YOUR EVOLVED LEADERSHIP JOURNEY

1. Which center of intelligence resonates most strongly for you when you think of what motivates your behaviors?

2. Think of a time at work when the impact of your behavior was not what you intended. How might the three centers of intelligence explain what happened?

3. What do you trust the most in stressful work situations: objective facts, feelings or impact on people, or your inner sense of what is the right thing? How is this different or similar to people you work closely with?

CHAPTER 4

UNDERSTANDING TRAUMA: YOUR PAST IS MORE PRESENT THAN YOU THINK

When I was in my twenties, one of my favorite TV shows was *ER* (short for Emergency Room).[1] Thursday nights at 10 p.m. were sacred—I looked forward to watching it all week, and there were very few times I was willing to skip it.

ER was a fast-paced drama that shared a mix of medical and personal stories with a behind-the-scenes view into the lives of the nurses, doctors, and support staff of a busy hospital in downtown Chicago. It had an ensemble cast, including two relatively unknown actors at the time, George Clooney and Anthony Edwards, and it managed to deftly combine lots of intense visuals, life complications, and famous guest appearances.

It was gory and gruesome one minute, with romantic tension the next. I loved it.

In almost every episode, in between conversations about cheating spouses or why the holiday decorations were still up, someone would shout, "Incoming trauma!" or the team would need to work quickly to revive an unconscious patient who had suffered blunt force trauma. The stories focused on patients with broken bones or horrific injuries, with the doctors racing against the clock to bring people back to life.

Seeing these injuries defined as trauma aligned with my lived understanding from my childhood when my mom would talk about the traumas she encountered at the hospital where she worked. She would come home and share the details from her day, which always involved difficult situations and stories of accidents and unexpected deaths.

As a result, I believed that trauma was a physical thing—a devastating injury to your body. You knew it was trauma because the injuries and symptoms were severe, often stemming from a single event. I learned later that there were other examples that could create long-term trauma, like child abuse, but I always equated trauma with a known physical injury.

Despite knowing that various sources of trauma existed, I never applied the term to anything that had happened in my own life. My relationship with my dad was tumultuous from when I was a young age, but it wasn't until I was in my twenties that I understood it was his substance abuse that created emotional havoc with him. But I never would have referred to it as trauma. It felt wrong to label it that way when I also enjoyed a level of privilege in my life.

It wasn't until recently during the pandemic that I realized how limited and outdated my perspective about trauma was. In reality, trauma is much more common.

While a physical injury can cause trauma, it's more complicated than that. Perhaps that is why it's a topic that's been avoided in leadership theory and reserved mainly for social scientists and physicians. I've come to understand there has been significant progress in the area of trauma research. This field has progressed tremendously in the past two decades, with important findings that shed light onto our relational abilities and patterns. I believe it's time to introduce it into leadership discussions, especially for proponents of human-based leadership.

And as we come through the biggest shared trauma in recent history, we need to better understand trauma and how it affects each of us in order to look at how leadership needs to change as a result of it.

WHAT IS TRAUMA?

As Dr. Gabor Maté notes in his book *The Myth of Normal*, "[T]he meaning of the word 'trauma,' in its Greek origin, is 'wound.' Whether we realize it or not, it is our woundedness, or how we cope with it, that dictates much of our behavior, shapes our social habits, and informs our ways of thinking about the world."[2] All of us carry these wounds from living our lives, but they play out in different ways in each of us.

These wounds lead to ongoing changes in how we behave in the present day. The Centre for Addiction and Mental Health (CAMH), one of the leading mental health organizations in Canada, defines trauma as "the lasting emotional response that often results from living through a distressing event."[3] We experience the traumatic event, survive it, but it continues to affect us, often without us realizing it.

Dr. Maté says that traumas are things that cause pain, and in my experience, no one likes talking about pain. We tend to only think of trauma as being the extreme and horrifying events in our lives. Dr. Maté defines such an event as a big-T trauma, "[which] occurs when things happen to vulnerable people that should not have happened, for example, a child being abused, or violence in the family, or a rancorous divorce, or the loss of a parent."[4] This "big-T" trauma is what most of us think of when we first understand trauma and understand it to be something that only happens to a small group of people at a certain point in time. The severity of big-T trauma is not questioned, and we do not judge others for suffering from its impact.

Examples of big-T trauma can include:

- Sexual assault
- Car accidents, even if without visible or lasting injuries
- Unplanned hospital stays or unexpected surgery complications
- Living in a country at war
- Losing a loved one to suicide
- Complications during childbirth (which can be traumatic for either parent)
- Witnessing an accident, fire, shooting, or other emergency event
- Extensive childhood abuse or neglect

This is how most of us think of trauma. We think of it as something that has happened, tragically, to a person in their past and understand that if left untreated, it can affect how someone behaves in their present life.

We rarely think about trauma as having other less drastic forms.

There's a more pervasive and much less understood version of trauma, which Maté calls small-t trauma. These are events where the level of critical injury may appear smaller, but the mind still associates it with fear, anger, or lack of safety.

Examples of small- or little-t trauma might look like:

- Missed diagnosis of a learning disability, or lack of support for cognitive issues from teachers and/or family
- Illness of a parent
- Moving frequently in childhood
- Microaggressions (e.g., repeatedly being asked to get coffee or take minutes because you're the only person of color on the team)
- Food, shelter, or safety insecurity as a child
- A manager with a demanding personality

I could go on and on.

The bottom line is that trauma will be different for each person. Even if two people experience the same event, their responses may significantly vary. And herein lies a devastating problem. Because our responses aren't the same in every situation, we can quickly jump to judgment and call people "lazy" or "not tough enough." Or, on the other end of the spectrum, we may easily label people who've tolerated extreme adversity as "tough cookies" or "warriors."

It's not helpful to anyone when we judge what is and what isn't trauma. We are not our traumas and labeling each other is destructive and ignorant.

Trauma exists when something happens that is too much for us to handle. How we define what is too much varies from person to person—what is too much for me might be enough for you to handle. It's why we shy away from using the word trauma—it feels nebulous, weighted down by opinions and tragedy. Why should you be able to consider your cancer experience as trauma when I got through my cancer diagnosis without complaint? Or when I don't refer to the neglect I faced in my childhood that way? Does that make me stronger and more capable? Are you weaker when you use it? The answer is no.

It can be difficult to wrap our heads around the idea that each of us may have faced some form of trauma or that we could be responding to what happened to us in varying degrees. We saw this in the aftermath of the first waves of COVID. We all faced the same event, including shared windows for lockdown, limited access to communal spaces, and isolation and anxiety about health risks, yet many other cognitive, emotional, and physical factors impacted how we felt about our collective experience. If we worked in public spaces like health care, education, transit, or food services; if we had small children or ailing parents; if we or our loved ones were immunocompromised; if we were already in emotionally or physically abusive relationships (or any number of additional factors), how we referred to our experience and how we felt was wide-ranging.

Simply stated, your body responds to perceived threats in physical, mental, and emotional ways. COVID is an example of a perceived physical threat. We experience mental and emotional threats in our working world as well as in our relationships. Despite their lack of physical impact, it doesn't make them any less devastating or change our body's desired response and interest in keeping us safe.

It's why we're seeing a number of different responses to return-to-office mandates. Some people feel they've come through the pandemic fairly easily and welcome a return to a regular routine. For others, working in their preferred home office environment for extended periods of time or potentially having dealt with crisis moments during periods of isolation have prompted a rethinking of their priorities.

The combination of traumatic events throughout someone's life can also have a compounding factor. Someone might not otherwise consider their experience with a confrontational boss as traumatic, but when combined with having a verbally abusive parent as a child, it could become overwhelming. As the CTRI notes, "Any experience of trauma can leave a person more vulnerable to experience a subsequent stressor as traumatic."[5]

Even if someone doesn't use the word *trauma*, it can still be felt as trauma in your mind and body. Whether the trauma we experience is small or large (by your own definition, not a global standard), it can have widespread impact. Childhood abuse survivors, for example, might recall traumatic events years later while still seeing it affect how they've formed relationships or experienced challenges with work or school. The word *trauma* is often left out when referring to the experience of cancer survivors, yet they might consider their experience with missed diagnoses, painful treatments, or lack of support to be similarly traumatic.

As leaders, the point here isn't to feel that you need to become experts in recognizing or diagnosing trauma. It's not your job to decide whether someone has experienced a big-T trauma or a smaller traumatic event, or even whether they might have experienced it at all. It's important to know that everyone has experienced some form of trauma in their life, even if only with the recent COVID pandemic.

Because you are human, you have experienced some form of wounding. If we are going to stand for human-centered leadership, then we must accept that trauma has impacted every one of us. That may seem daunting, unnecessary, and too heavy. Having awareness, however, is the first step in behavior change and bringing more compassion into leadership.

TRAUMA SPECIFICS: THREE TYPES OF TRAUMAS

Just like there are big-T and small-t traumas, there are different types of traumas stemming from their sources. Trauma research has made significant progress in the past twenty years with the help of researchers including Gabor Maté, Peter Levine, Resmaa Menakem, and Shaili Jain. While their work points to a number of types of traumas, when we look at workplace impacts, there are three main types of traumas that can impact how people work together.

> **Situational trauma** – the impact to a person as a result of a singular or repeated challenging event.
>
> **Racialized trauma** – the impact to a person as a result of racism, from significant events and/or smaller, repeated, pervasive events.
>
> **Collective trauma** – the impact to a large group of people, including employees at a company, inhabitants of the same town or city, or larger, global groups facing a similar threat or difficult challenge.

Not everyone can point to a situational or racialized trauma event. However, we have all experienced a collective trauma with the COVID pandemic. The combination of uncertainty, changing circumstances and upheaval from remote work, children moving between remote and in-person learning, access to food and medicine, illness and death of loved ones, missed milestones like weddings and graduations, the inability to mourn in a healthy way, a lack of positive experiences like trips, family events, and parties—it was a trauma soup that we all tumbled into and struggled to find our way through. And it happened to all of us at the same time with the pandemic. No one could buy or bribe their way out of it; it stopped us in our tracks.

Then the murder of George Floyd occurred. Trauma dominated the headlines and forced us to confront uncomfortable truths in our society and our workplaces.

Each of us has elements from our life that are traumatic, to different degrees. If you are human, you have trauma.

The amount of adaptation and change people were being asked to work through in the workplace, on top of the pandemic impact itself, was immense. And we're still dealing with its consequences today.

Even if we don't realize that we've experienced trauma in our past, difficult events in our present day can trigger a trauma response. As research from the CTRI notes, "when a person's sense of well-being and survival is threatened, instincts kick in, setting off a traumatic stress response. The source of this experience may be a particular incident, an interaction or a series of events that create an atmosphere that is destabilizing."[6]

When health authorities declared that our best defense against COVID was to stay isolated, responses ranged from immediate compliance to absolute defiance. Being forced into a situation like this with no warning, no precedent, and no clear ending in sight was very destabilizing. We had no control over the situation and there was no room for modified approaches. That doesn't create a feeling of safety in our nervous systems.

You might not realize that an event can trigger a trauma response in another person and can completely take over a person's ability to stay or respond appropriately in the situation. Even long after the traumatic event occurs, it can be revived again instantly if a person feels even the smallest amount of danger or perceives a threat.[7]

These definitions of trauma might be familiar to you, but they unlocked a whole new world for me. My resistance to the word *trauma* at this point was clearly an indicator of my ability to process it. I had protected myself with unhealthy overworking and perfectionistic behaviors to shield myself from dealing with my own trauma. When the pandemic hit, I was calm and thankful that I had "global permission" to rest. My coping mechanisms up until this point had looked after me, and my body could activate old patterns so that I could withstand the emotional landslide that had fallen upon us. It was keeping me stuck, and I didn't know what else to do other than push through it.

I don't want you to feel that this means you need to become an expert in psychology or understand who on your team has experienced trauma. Rather, I want you to understand that some of the people on your team have experienced situational and/or racialized trauma, and all of them (including you) have experienced collective trauma from the pandemic.

Whether they themselves understand that they've experienced trauma isn't needed.

THE DIFFERENCE BETWEEN STRESS AND TRAUMA

All traumatic events are stressful, but not all stressful events are traumatic.[8]

Every day at work, people face stressful situations. Stress is a natural reaction when your body is facing a change or a disturbance to your routine. Your heart rate will increase, breathing will become faster, and you might have sharpened senses. Your body releases cortisol and adrenaline to deal with the threat. It can be a positive response, keeping you alert and focused, but it can be harmful to your body if it happens too often or for too long.

For thousands of years, our brain has worked hard to protect us from threats. Back in the Stone Age, our threats were physical in nature, which helped us avoid being dinner for a predator. Now our threats are not only physical, but they are also mental and emotional as well.

When stress is continual, the body doesn't get the chance to return to a normal, regulated state where your breathing and heart rate are calmly paced. This leads to dysregulation. Physically, your heart rate stays elevated, blood pressure can increase, and breathing becomes fast and shallow, among other things. Difficult thoughts and feelings can take over, making moods and reactions unpredictable. When your daily life is disturbed on a continual basis like this, it is chronic stress.

According to research cited in *Harvard Business Review*, workplace stress is estimated to cost the US economy more than 500 billion dollars, and each year, 550 million work days are lost due to stress on the job.[9]

It's not much wonder with so much volatility, uncertainty, and ambiguity in our world, many of us are living with dysregulated nervous systems. We're on guard all the time, and our body is stuck in a constant state of hypervigilance.

A healthy amount of stress is good for you, but chronic stress is not. With chronic stress, your body never returns to its normal state (referred to as homeostasis), and it can end up engaging the nervous system's trauma response.

WE STORE TRAUMA IN OUR BODIES

When we're afraid, we struggle to solve problems, be innovative, feel safe, or provide psychological safety to others. If this fear is traumatic, it doesn't go away when the triggering fear is resolved; our bodies remember this fear so we can be prepared if the danger occurs again.

None of this is under our conscious control—it's happening in our body automatically. The part of our brain that processes and regulates emotions (the limbic system) gets hyper-aroused from the fear, and it shuts down access to the part of our brain responsible for thinking, problem solving, and integration (also called the prefrontal cortex). That means our emotional reaction to an event may be over the top as our thoughts and emotions become muddled. Dr. Dan Siegel, a clinical psychology professor, coined the term "flipping your lid" to describe this process and created a hand model visualization to make it simple to see what is taking place in the brain.[10] I've included his YouTube video in my Resource section at the end of the book.

In 1995, physician Bessel van der Kolk started to question the existing treatment for trauma patients. In his groundbreaking book *The Body Keeps the Score*, he provided proof that trauma can't be fully treated by talking because so much of our trauma is stored in our bodies.

This is consistent with the progress of trauma research and the shift from a cognitive understanding of trauma (that it's "in our heads") to an understanding that it has somatic elements as well, where the impact of trauma is also felt and stored in our bodies. As a result, trauma isn't something we can think our way out of; it's buried in our bodies. This is a major shift in accurately understanding the impact of trauma.

Throughout my life, I believed I was handling life's adversities just fine by being strong and tough, but my body was telling me a different story.

The first time my body sounded the alarm was when I was in my midtwenties. Out of the blue I started experiencing digestive issues without an obvious cause. I couldn't tolerate much food, and it would pass right through me. I could usually manage soup, but that was about it. Some days, I couldn't eat anything.

Rapid weight loss followed, which was no surprise, as I was hardly able to keep anything down. More than 40 pounds dropped off my 5′10″ frame, and I was at a gaunt 110 pounds. I felt unwell, and no one could figure out what was causing it. I was tested for every possible illness, from Crohn's to colitis to cancer. I had colonoscopies, X-rays, all kinds of poking and prodding. But no one could figure it out.

I didn't realize it at the time, but in looking back, my body was in a heightened state of fear. I was trying to outrun a contentious situation with my father by cutting him out of my life, something I had never dared to try before. On top of that, I was searching for my first "grown-up" job, having just completed five years of university where I earned two degrees. Rent was too expensive while I was living with my friend, so I moved in with my uncle. My mom had relocated back to the Maritimes a year earlier, and I wasn't prepared to move to a different province. All this uncertainty was undoubtedly stressful, but the conflict with my father was unbearable.

Fast-forward several months. I was in a new romantic relationship with the man who would become my future husband. I felt safe and secure. And just as suddenly as it began, I was able to keep food down. My weight returned to healthy levels, and I started to feel like myself once again. That's when I realized that maybe my body was trying to tell me something: "Hey Carolyn, you thought some things were in the past, but we're here to remind you that you haven't dealt with them yet."

We have a faulty belief that when we walk through the doors or open our computers on a workday that we're able to direct ourselves cognitively to do what needs to be done. But the thing with our nervous system is that it has stored memories in our body in order to protect us from future threats, and we never know when they might show up.

Our bodies constantly watch for stressors, and as authors Ball and Siegel note, "when trauma threatens your well-being, it affects your *whole* being—your body, heart, and mind" (emphasis theirs).[11] This is why we covered centers of intelligence before diving into trauma. Our bodies, our hearts, and our minds are affected by trauma, and we aren't always aware that we are responding to perceived threats.

The biggest shift we need to make is understanding that our trauma responses don't happen cognitively from our brains; they happen physiologically from our bodies. Trauma disrupts our ability to use each center (head, heart, and body) fully and equally.

This matters because at work, we expect that everyone will respond rationally in every situation. We expect people to handle the news of layoffs calmly, then willingly follow the procedural steps that are laid out. We ask that people take the news of policy changes that affect salary or benefits "like adults" and stay detached from emotion. We monitor our employees for keystrokes and other data points that prove they're staying at their desks, despite evidence that moving your body can help your brain.

Similarly, we have unrealistic expectations that trauma responses should have a fixed end date, with a reduced or eliminated response after an "appropriate" amount of time. Trauma is stored in the lower limbic system of our brain, which has no concept of time. If the stress is remembered and carried in our body, we might react the following day or forty years later. The notion that we should be "over it by now" is irrelevant.

Stress is a part of life but too many of us push through, suck it up, and grind it out. We overlook the wisdom in our body, especially when we're feeling tired and overburdened. As a result, our centers of intelligence become less integrated and don't operate to their fullest potential.

It becomes a badge of honor to overcome our shortage of time by using "hacks" to be increasingly productive and check more things off our list. Our bodies are glorious, yet most of us are not treating them well. This is more than managing your physical fitness. To fully integrate and balance our centers of intelligence, we need to know more about regulating our nervous system. That's what we'll discuss in the next chapter.

REFLECTIONS ON YOUR EVOLVED LEADERSHIP JOURNEY

1. How would you describe the stress in your life? Is it chronic? Are physical symptoms present?

2. Did you learn anything new about trauma in this chapter? Were any myths debunked?

3. What's your initial reaction to the word trauma? What thoughts come to mind? What feelings arise? What sensations unfold in your body?

CHAPTER 5

OUR NERVOUS SYSTEMS ARE SHELL-SHOCKED

In March 2020 when the COVID-19 pandemic was declared, I was ready. I didn't panic or flinch. There were lots of rumors flying around the internet about shortages of hospital beds and equipment and high rates of infection, but I was surprised to discover that I wasn't worried or anxious about it.

Instead, I felt calm and prepared. "This isn't my first pandemic," I kept repeating to myself. "I know what to do."

Of course, it wasn't that I'd gone through an *actual* pandemic at an earlier point in my life. Perhaps I wasn't as calm as I thought I was. Maybe I was returning to a known state I had gone to for previous traumas. A calm, collected approach that fooled me into thinking I had it all under control.

I will pause and acknowledge that my personal situation through the pandemic was one of privilege. My family and I were safe in a house that could hold all of us comfortably. I didn't lose anyone close to me from the virus. My business was able to rapidly pivot to virtual program delivery. All good things.

Others in a similar situation did struggle emotionally and mentally. They found it difficult to cope with the continued uncertainty and confusing information online. They argued with their families after being cooped up. They worried about their kids bringing the virus home from school.

I was able to stay calm. This was one situation that didn't trigger too many chronic stress responses in me.

There were clearly events in my childhood that were traumatic, events that unfolded when I was alone with my dad during scheduled biweekly visits that I was afraid to tell anyone about. Moments like paying my dad's bar bill as a ten-year-old, or when he used me as a shield in a bar fight, or my paying his overdue rent so he wouldn't get kicked out of his home, a motel room. And then there were those times I hesitated over getting into the car because I thought he'd had too much to drink. But I didn't see a problem with any of these situations. It was simply my reality, and I thought I was strong enough to deal with it on my own.

Early experiences shape how we deal with adversity later in life. These become learned behaviors we repeat because we think they are serving us. When we become trauma-informed leaders, we understand that trauma in one's past can affect how one behaves today, and thus, being compassionate becomes much easier.

When we try to become more vulnerable because we're told it's the secret to greater levels of engagement and work satisfaction, we find ourselves unable to do so, or we aren't clear about what exactly is needed from us. When we can't be our true selves at work, when we're hiding the pain and stress from the traumas or challenges we've faced, our bodies sense this lack of safety and shift into protective mode. We stay stuck in a perpetual mode of hiding and pretending, and we see it pop up when we're pushed into a corner. We stay stuck in a heightened state of fear (because that's what our body remembers), and in that fear state, we're unable to access the deeper level of thinking and problem solving we need. We'll talk more about protective behaviors in Chapter 7.

WHAT TRAUMA DOES TO OUR NERVOUS SYSTEM

When our bodies sense stress and connect it to trauma in our past (or even a difficult singular stressful event), we can respond without being cognitively aware that we're doing so. Being under stress in this way makes our vision myopic—we become short-sighted and struggle to see the bigger picture.

What does this look like at work? It could look like being put on the spot in a meeting when you're asked a question you're unsure about how to answer because your body is remembering an earlier time when your manager laughed at your response in front of your team members. You freeze because you don't want to make the same mistake, and your brain becomes fixated on that moment without being able to pull back and recognize that the situation you're in is vastly different.

When our bodies feel under threat, how we respond might look excessive or extreme to others. We're experiencing an amygdala hijack, a phrase first coined by Dr. Daniel Goleman, where our brain is responding on the level of perceived threat, pushing us to respond as if its perception of our situation is our reality. In the aforementioned example of freezing in a meeting when you feel fear of being criticized, an amygdala hijack could trigger you to quit on the spot and walk out the door. The response seems extreme and possibly dramatic to others, but in the moment, it feels completely rational and reasonable to you because it removes you from the imminent threat. This is an example of "flipping your lid," a concept I introduced in Chapter 4.

Our responses to stress can take our nervous system out of regulation to varying degrees. It might be slightly dysregulated, where we feel irritated and can't shake it off, or we might get to a state of hyperarousal and get visibly angry. It's possible that dysregulation in our nervous system can go the other way too, where we withdraw, appearing cold or numb to others. If this happens to a significant degree in a state of hypoarousal, this can look like indifference to others but is a protective mechanism to prevent us from getting emotionally invested in something that could harm us.

Our goal is to build the skills that keep us more consistently regulated and less inclined to go into states of extreme agitation. As we'll talk about in Chapter 10, building the skills and practices to expand range (called your window of tolerance—another term coined by Dan Siegel), and your ability to stay calm and regulated during times of stress is a critical skill that leaders need to build post-pandemic.

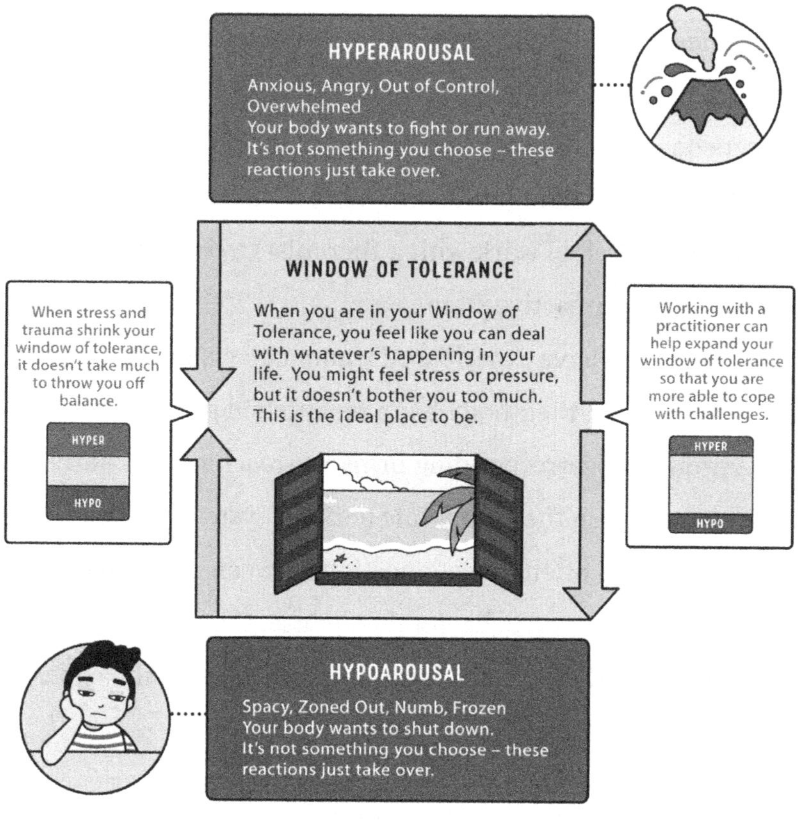

https://www.nicabm.com/trauma-how-to-help-your-clients-understand-their-window-of-tolerance/[1]

Your teams need to see that they can count on you as their leader to stay reasonable and rational through all the uncertainty and upheaval they're facing. Understanding your own window of tolerance gives you the awareness to stay calm. With coaching and/or therapy, you can also work to increase the range of your window, which is especially helpful if your range is small.

There's added complexity to acknowledge. Not everyone will respond to their past trauma in the same way, even if the events were similar. Siegel notes that for people who have experienced trauma, triggering events can pull them out of their ability to cope more easily than someone who isn't triggered by that event.[1] We might move more readily to freeze or flight because of our past trauma, and it will take new skills (or possibly work with a therapist) to increase our ability to remain in an unreactive state.

For people who have experienced trauma, to whatever degree feels significant to them, their body has a heightened sense of danger and may be prone to overresponding or hyper-reactivity. As author Deb Dana notes, "[w]hen the autonomic nervous system has been shaped by trauma, there is often a disconnection between physiological state, psychological story, and behavioral response. Cues of danger seem to be everywhere and the smallest reminder of a traumatic experience activates a survival response."[2]

Perhaps this is behind the excessive reaction you experienced with someone at work.

Remember, it's not your job to assess why someone acted a certain way or to label it as a trauma response. But if you want to be an evolved leader, then it is your responsibility to be compassionate and less judgmental because that instills a sense of safety.

As Bessel van der Kolk's research highlights, the learned responses to trauma are how the body learns to cope, filing it away as a way to prepare for a future traumatic event. He notes, "trauma is not just an event that took place sometime in the past; it is also the imprint left by that experience on mind, brain, and body. This imprint has ongoing consequences for how the human organism manages to survive in the present."[3]

Pause and take that in. Think of the vast number of people around you impacted by the pandemic alone—physically, mentally, and/or emotionally.

It's worth repeating that trauma isn't a cognitive experience. Trauma is stored unconsciously in your body so your nervous system can keep watch and protect you from that threat.

When your body experiences too much stress and perceives danger, it moves into action to protect you. In this state, connection with others decreases and threat activation increases. These are known as the 4 Fs.

Fight – take charge and remove the danger before it gets you; instinct is to act aggressively

Flight – escape danger; instinct is to leave the situation and avoid conflict

Fawn – seek approval and appease others to avoid conflict and/or threat; instinct is to rely on others present to make choices or decisions

Freeze – the highest level of threat activation; instinct is to do nothing and not move or act; unable to function under pressure

These responses are built into our nervous system to handle short-term threat surges. They keep us safe, so it's important to learn and honor them. It also gives you the opportunity to elevate awareness about potential chronic stress patterns and understand the wisdom your body is trying to share with you. At work, these responses could look like the following:

Fight might look like arguing in a meeting, slamming doors, or taking opposing sides to issues. One can feel intense anger, be overly aggressive, insult others, or have a desire to blame others. On the positive side, it can help us be assertive and stand up for what's right and help us feel courageous.

Flight might look like skipping a meeting or taking sick leave or longer breaks. When this happens, one can feel breathless, flighty, fidgety, mouth dryness, or anxiety. It might look like being busy all the time as well. This response helps us avoid harmful conversations and prevents physical danger.

Fawn might look like easy agreement or being quiet during team decisions or being overly flattering to teammates or managers. This means it's hard to say no, and one can seem excessively polite and helpful. This response can help build unity on a team and demonstrate the benefits of being unselfish.

Freeze might look like no longer responding to emails or avoiding or declining meetings unexpectedly. The body enters a state of energy conversation, making it difficult to think and make decisions. One can feel dread or a desire to hide, and sometimes numbness occurs. Helpful aspects of this response include sharp hearing, good awareness of surroundings, and being in the present moment.

If we've been traumatized, we're more likely to activate one of these responses in times of perceived trauma. With chronic stress or unresolved trauma, the nervous system becomes dysregulated, and this threat system meant to protect us becomes overactive. It's like having a fire alarm go off every time you cook in the kitchen when you only need it to activate when there's smoke.

When we experience trauma stress responses in our body, it's like we've gone back in time. As author Nadine Burke Harris writes in *The Deepest Well*, "[t]he problem with PTSD is that it becomes entrenched; the stress response is caught in the past, stuck on repeat."[4] We find ourselves repeating patterns of behavior that are unexpected or even undetectable to us because we do them as if on autopilot. These are indicators of dysregulation and possibly even a stress response to past trauma, especially if they are happening often.

- Have you ever found yourself getting angry in a meeting and not knowing why?
- Are you exploding emotionally onto people at work, or feeling close to it?
- Are you pushing the pace so fast that it seems you're the only one who can keep up?
- Do you feel you're letting people down because you don't have the answer they're looking for?
- Do you find yourself automatically apologizing when asked a question?
- Are you frustrated with teammates because they never have the right answer, so you take on their tasks?
- Are you giving up on participating in meetings because it's too hard to keep up or you just don't care anymore?
- Do you feel compelled to defend your position or react in the chat while someone is making a point?
- Does turning off your camera for virtual meetings feel more comfortable?

The physical responses to stress make connecting to our body center of intelligence all the more critical. As we'll talk about in Chapters 9 and 10, there are practices we can do daily that help keep our nervous systems regulated, even coregulated when we're in conversations with others.

As leaders, it isn't our job to fix or work to expand someone's ability to tolerate stressful events or expand their tolerance window; we need to focus on regulating our own responses and staying out of judgment. We'll dive into more detail about this in Chapter 9.

GAPS WHEN WE DON'T ACCESS BODY INTELLIGENCE

In the past, leadership books haven't typically focused on somatic practices (connecting the mind to physical responses in the body, such as pain, discomfort, hesitation, etc.) as being an important part of analyzing and understanding what skills we need to lead well. We've stepped into understanding the importance of mindfulness, but we connect it more to "slowing/improving the mind" than having a broader awareness of the importance of connecting to what's happening and what we're feeling in our body. We're disconnected from ourselves.

If we can't connect our mind and body properly and understand the signals our body is sending us to try and protect us, it further impacts our ability to successfully connect to others as well.

Being a trauma-informed leader does not require you at any time to use talk therapy or try to resolve a problem someone is facing. That's the job of a professional. But as a leader, you can create an environment that doesn't cause unnecessary anxiety and can create a feeling of safety. This is what being trauma-informed is all about.

Our body responds unconsciously to its environment, trying to keep it safe and protected. And there are feelings we have stored in our bodies that are going to react, regardless of our consciousness about them.

RECOGNIZING TRAUMA IN OURSELVES AND OTHERS

It's a lot. Understanding that difficulties from our past could still be affecting our present-day behavior can be frustrating and overwhelming, especially if we thought we'd overcome them. You might be thinking, *yes, that awful thing happened to me, but I haven't thought about it in years*. Or maybe, *I've learned how to manage my body language to make sure no one knows it happened*. Or maybe you don't even know it happened.

These statements can be true AND you may still be seeing the effects of trauma in your life without even realizing it. It's likely too soon after the start of the pandemic to know the full extent of how it's impacting you and the people around you.

How do we begin to acknowledge that the effects of trauma may be affecting us and our colleagues, friends, and family?

A major step forward is changing the narrative and language from "what's wrong with you?" to considering "what has happened to you?" The CTRI calls this taking our thoughts from judgment to curiosity,[5] where we move from thinking behaviors we dislike in ourselves and others stem from an illness or intentional disregard for acceptable social norms to understanding that these behaviors likely have trauma incidents at their core and thus require trauma-informed responses from others.

An example I see frequently is when managers get frustrated with employees who prefer working from home and they react with a statement like: "What is wrong with that person? Why can't they just come into the office two days a week? That's not a big ask, and they did it before the pandemic." A less reactive statement that creates more opportunity for connection would be: "I wonder what I can do as their manager to help with this transition into a different working environment."

I didn't understand chronic stress, nor did I understand trauma. I worked hard to the point of exhaustion and overperformance, which I now see as both fight and fawn responses. I was avoiding the discomfort of pain by keeping busy and combining it with a desire to work my way up the ladder as proof that I was getting through it okay.

I had no idea how to listen to my body and understand what it was trying to tell me. Clearly, I had missed a few of these signals along the way. So where do you start in learning how to leverage the intelligence of your body center? Resmaa Menakem, author of several books on racialized trauma, has coined the acronym VIMBAS to define the different forms of body intelligence that we can rely on to interpret stress responses.[6] These six categories include:

Vibrations – the energy your body feels

Images or thoughts – words or visuals that come to mind, including ideas, visions, or memories

Meanings – our interpretations from past events, including stories, conclusions, or explanations

Behaviors, impulses, and urges – how your body acts or wants to act

Affect and emotions – joy, fear, sadness, anxiety, etc.

Sensations – cold or heat, tingles, tightness or pressure, etc.

You've likely sensed one or all these responses. Now that you have validation that they give you important signals to keep your nervous system regulated, you can trust them and build your ability to sense them and hear your body when it's talking to you.

We've learned about the nervous system, regulation, and dysregulation, and how our body responds to perceived threats through fight, flight, fawn, and freeze. You can appreciate why creating safety is an important area of focus for evolved leaders.

It's so critical that we're going to expand on it in the next chapter.

REFLECTIONS ON YOUR EVOLVED LEADERSHIP JOURNEY

1. How would you describe your own window of tolerance? How might it impact your effectiveness as a leader?

2. Which of the 4 Fs gets activated in you when you're stressed?

3. Which of the VIMBAS are you able to access most readily? Which ones might you try developing?

CHAPTER 6

WHEN WE CAN'T BE OUR TRUE SELVES AT WORK

My kids learned to do laundry and make their own lunches earlier than most—a survival strategy for me so I wasn't engulfed by domestic chores when I was a widowed single mom. As teenagers, my boys' independence went to a whole new level with places they needed to be, and I was simply the part-time chauffeur. I didn't mind most of the time. It was an opportunity to connect and provide emotional support without having to stare eye to eye, which can feel awkward, especially for teenage boys.

Soon though, they could drive or get a ride from friends, and opportunities for the impromptu talks disappeared. Working from home then became a huge benefit. My kids could wander into my office anytime if they needed anything. Emotional support doesn't usually fit into a schedule, so it was handy being around when the moment struck.

By this time, my business was well established, and I had developed a few partnerships. With the boys around less, I committed to additional projects and traveled more, taking on a range of responsibilities. I was focusing more deeply on the evidence to support my client work, including examining the research that underpinned healthy workplace cultures and human-centered leadership.

There are blurred memories from this time; I think I've blocked some of it out because it was incredibly difficult to juggle everyone's needs, both at work and at home, all while I was unaware of the feelings simmering inside me.

Old patterns emerged, and my capacity to take on incredible amounts of work was on full display. I didn't want to say no to any partnerships and felt responsible for everything from operations to client work to sales. No one asked me to take all this on, and I chalked it up as living the values of radical responsibility and accountability.

The pressure at home ballooned as well. My boys, who had coped well when they lost their father, struggled through new grief milestones as teenagers. And then there were the hardships of blending families. My coping mechanism was to take swift action and find solutions for everyone else without pausing or looking inward and considering my own reactions.

The same pattern showing up again.

LIFE IN THE PRETENDING ZONE

Author Haruki Murakami notes, "[s]ometimes it's not the people who change, it's the mask that falls off."[1]

We now often wear physical masks in our workspaces, but the metaphorical ones are still there and we're still pretending we're okay. Even though we recognize saying we're "fine" isn't always convincing, we typically say it when someone asks how we are. And when we hear "fine" from others, it's often heard as a request to keep things on the surface and accept the answer at face value.

Lately, perhaps everyone is too exhausted to make the effort to ask any follow-up questions to better understand how someone is really feeling. It's a dance we do together in the spirit of keeping up the pretense that we're all getting through our pain and difficulties or ignoring that they even exist.

By comparison, sometimes things swing far the other way. You're having a conversation with someone in the office, and the next thing you know, they are sharing their deepest, darkest secrets. You're confused. What's going on? We're at work. What's happening? Do I have to share back? Do they realize this conversation is making me feel uncomfortable? How can I extract myself without hurting the other person's feelings? It gets awkward, fast. Our fear of exactly this situation is why we're happy with the more traditional "fine" answer.

Sound familiar? Unfortunately, variations of this situation often arise. When it happens, people might refer to it as being vulnerable, a quality that exudes authenticity and that research has proven elevates leadership, especially in these chaotic times. In fact, research by Brené Brown conducted years before the pandemic showed that CEOs believed courage was the only way their companies could survive through so much change and disruption. And the way courage showed up in their organizations? Through leaders who embraced vulnerability, had hard conversations, and pushed through the discomfort.

Let's be clear: pouring out your personal life to someone else and assuming it will build a stronger connection is not an act of vulnerability. It's oversharing. Some people may connect to it but frankly, it's not appropriate to overshare at work, and more so, it's not vulnerability. Remember the definition from Chapter 1? Vulnerability is "an emotion we experience when we cannot control the outcome and when there is uncertainty, risk and emotional exposure."[2]

An appropriate example of vulnerability is based on one's ability to stay open and curious when the outcome of an interaction is unknown and there is risk of being judged. At work, it could be in a meeting where you shared an opinion that differed from your boss's that led to engaging in a meaningful discussion without being judgmental or standing down. You didn't know what the outcome of the conversation would be, but you pushed through the discomfort, sharing a contrary opinion by believing in yourself.

Avoiding vulnerability is a natural reaction because it can feel uncomfortable or unsafe. Embracing the unknown can be hard, especially if the protection system we learned about in the last chapter is activated. As well, it's important to point out that being vulnerable is a choice and it isn't always a safe option. It's necessary to exercise discernment in who you are vulnerable with.

Research by Brené Brown shows that we fall prey to several myths about vulnerability that prevent us from leveraging it in our leadership. Every time I facilitate a Dare to Lead™ program, leaders struggle with letting go of their deeply held belief that vulnerability is a weakness. And I can understand why when power and control appear to be fundamental to achieving success.

Reframing what "vulnerability" means and creating a new relationship with it will transform you as a leader. You can embrace it with intention, move through the discomfort, and stay connected to your peers, colleagues, and teammates at work, which is not easy to do when we are being asked to deliver with certainty on business performance and time is at a premium.

Here's another situation that may sound familiar. You're in a meeting with a group of people, trying to solve a difficult issue. One person shares a personal story about why this issue has been difficult for them, and they have tears in their eyes. People respond by saying, "Wow, that's so vulnerable. Thanks for sharing." Again, a similar example of when we misunderstand what vulnerability means at work—that crying and sharing our personal details is a requirement to be a leader.

Proactively creating a safe space will invite vulnerable discussions, so it's important for leaders to identify guidelines and boundaries for the conversation. A few years ago, I attended an online training session in a group of fifty people. Managing a group that large online isn't easy, and I appreciated the efforts of the two facilitators. To kick off the session and build connection, they invited people to introduce themselves. One participant jumped in right away and shared a deeply personal story about how they'd recently lost their spouse. The chat box filled up with comments that applauded this person for being so vulnerable in sharing their story.

I didn't say anything. I was frustrated that the facilitators hadn't set clear instructions for us. Having individual introductions for fifty people was a mistake to start with and now other people felt as if they needed to introduce themselves on similarly personal levels. I was angry for the rest of the training. Part of me felt like a jerk—I could truly empathize with the pain this person was feeling about losing a spouse—and yet all I could think about was how angry I was to have been put in this position of being pushed to offer condolences in the chat box.

When I thought back on it later with the added lens of understanding trauma, I realized my reaction was in response to unhealed trauma and unresolved grief. If the facilitators had been mindful of leading in a trauma-informed way, they could have established guidelines, shared more precise directions, and avoided a number of issues in how the introductions unfolded. In Chapter 9, I'll provide more examples for how leaders can do so.

In recent years, much attention has been paid to psychological safety within teams. Psychological safety creates a sense of belonging and proper conditions to support vulnerability. The term, created by professor and researcher Amy Edmondson, is the absence of fear of unfair consequences at work.[3] As we're learning, creating physical and emotional safety in the workplace goes beyond a to-do list mentality; it needs to be part of the leader's mindset in how you show up day to day with your team—being open and transparent so your team can trust your word and actions. Without trust and a deep sense of safety, your team will continue to feel uncertain about their place at work or confident that they can operate effectively, both of which impact the overall effectiveness and success of the team.

TRAUMA PREVENTS VULNERABILITY

When I reflect on my time as a corporate leader, I realize now how much I avoided vulnerability. It might not have appeared that way, but the fact was that I avoided tough conversations and did everything I could to sidestep judgment and blame when it came to my work performance. People assumed that because I was open about discussing my personal life, it meant I was comfortable being vulnerable. That is not vulnerability; it's just comfort with disclosure.

The closer I got to the top of the organizational hierarchy, the harder it was to minimize conflict. It was unpredictable and felt very unsafe for me. At these leadership levels, you need to be objective and discerning. Respectful discourse and differences of opinion are critical to success and mitigating risk. It's not good if everyone agrees, but it certainly felt more comfortable for me.

When you're a leader, people watch every move you make, gauge your reactions, and look for patterns. It's the consistency of your reactivity that determines how people will show up under your leadership—open and authentic or cautious and guarded.

A few years after my Dare to Lead™ training with Brené Brown, I pulled out my notes and discovered a powerful quote. Brown said, "one of the biggest casualties of trauma is the inability to be vulnerable."[4] I had highlighted the quote and put stars around it. My subconscious must have known how pivotal it would be in my work, but I didn't grasp it at the time. As we infuse the importance of vulnerability into our leadership practices, it will serve us well to understand that vulnerability is not easily accessed by everyone.

Trauma responses happen when we are guarding against an uncertain outcome. Physiologically, we sense that the situation is unsafe, and we trigger our nervous system to prepare us to act. Whether this is to leave (flight), to battle (fight), to be immobile (freeze), or to distract (fawn), we are telling our bodies to be on alert for danger.

If vulnerability means being open to emotional risks even if the outcome is uncertain, a past traumatic experience can prevent us from being willing to be vulnerable.

If a workplace dynamic has previously been combative—people bluntly sharing difficult feedback without concern for the other person (often couched as being "open and transparent")—and the leadership team decides that this needs to change, it takes a significant amount of practice and unlearning to prevent guarding while allowing trauma-response triggers to subside.

While denial might feel like a personal coping mechanism, pretending the issues we faced personally during the height of the pandemic doesn't mean they've gone away; in addition to the same personal and family elements we were juggling pre-pandemic, our feelings about hybrid work environments elicit mixed feelings depending on our personal situations. We seemed to be more willing to respect the personal needs and values of individuals during the pandemic but stopped when the pandemic seemed to be "over." The effects of the pandemic don't go away overnight; we're seeing this in the change in conversations about the individual's relationship with work and through a shift in priorities.

THE DISSONANCE IS DRAINING US

I'm certified by Barrett Values Centre as a Cultural Transformation Certified Practitioner, which means I have helped many organizations in defining their values and engaging their employees in the process. Values are important for organizations to declare, as they provide alignment and clarity in how work gets done.

Here's what I've observed doing this work with clients: the same values are desired by every single organization, and it doesn't matter if they are nonprofit, member-based, corporate, government, or small businesses. They might vary in their wording, but the themes are essentially the same.

Accountability – includes concepts like reliability and dependability

Integrity – doing the right thing; being ethical

Adaptability – also referred to as innovation, continuous learning, or agility

Collaboration – sometimes described as teamwork
Inclusivity – before 2020, it was usually integrated into collaboration and now is exclusively identified
Excellence – dedication to high standards for the product or service

While these are admirable values, they aren't always inspiring behavior change or bringing alignment to teams as they navigate their business challenges.

With all my clients, we identify behaviors that define "what good looks like" and what "wrong looks like" for each value. This is co-created with leaders and employees so everyone's voice is heard. Surprisingly, this exercise is stressful for some leaders. They worry that if we let the employees take control, they won't pick the right behaviors. That hasn't happened. Ever.

It should be pretty straightforward for everyone to live the values when behaviors are clearly articulated, right?

Nope. There are many leaders who aren't seeing their teams demonstrate the company's values, and on the flip side, there are employees who aren't seeing their managers leading in alignment with these values either. We seem to think it is a binary "yes or no" checkbox to living the values, without understanding the deeper nuances at play.

The missing piece here is vulnerability. Values need openness, empathy, compassion, and communication if they are going to be more than words on paper. For those leaders who worried about the wrong values being picked, it was the discomfort of vulnerability talking.

Values aren't rule books. They are guideposts to help employees in organizations make aligned decisions. The good behaviors we want to encourage and the bad behaviors we want to prevent. However, there's a gap between good and bad. It's the gray area where interpretation can vary; this is where tension lies and where meaningful exploration about values exists.

Remember high school science when you learned that inside tension lies potential energy? When there is tension on a team, there is an opportunity to harness that tension by engaging in conversation, in a vulnerable discussion, where all parties share their perspective. This is the optimal way to use tension and bring the values to life.

Unfortunately, the tension is often avoided, it's uncomfortable, or there isn't enough time, so energy is wasted. Sometimes the tension explodes and stretches people too far, which causes relational damage. Either way, leaders need to accept the discomfort and leverage the tension.

It's no secret that trust is the glue that keeps teams together and performing at a strong level. When trust is low, a team's ability to leverage the tension is seriously compromised. Then it becomes a vicious cycle where people wait for more trust before they are prepared to be vulnerable.

I see this type of situation playing out over and over again in my work. People willingly step into the work of practicing vulnerability in our training sessions or expressing deeply felt commitments to upholding a new set of shared values. They are heartfelt in the moment, and I know they believe the changes they are determined to make are genuine. And yet invariably, weeks or months later when I circle back to the group or leaders who initiated the work, I'll hear the same stories of how difficult it is to act differently when they're back at work.

Vulnerability is uncomfortable and hard, especially if we don't feel a strong sense of psychological safety.

When we aren't living or working in alignment with our values or our values aren't reflected in our work or workplaces, our energy levels take a toll. Through the work of Tony Schwartz, we know leaders prefer to manage work by focusing on time, not outcomes.[5] We saw this at the start of the pandemic, with leaders asking for tools to better monitor how much time people were working in their new work-from-home environments. The *New York Times* featured a podcast on workforce surveillance tools—keystroke tracking tools used to monitor employees' idle time away from their keyboards—to keep track of how productive people were while working from home.[6] These tools entirely missed all the important work that people were performing as they read long-form articles, reports, or spreadsheets they had printed, and even time in deep discussions with clients or colleagues. In some cases, people weren't being paid for any time that couldn't be mapped back to keyboard use, even though much of that time is equally (or more) valuable.

It's no wonder we struggle with implementing values when we're trying to force them through by only engaging our head centers and resisting the vulnerable conversations driven by our heart centers. If we aren't examining our work from all angles and determining where there's dissonance to the new values we set, we will struggle to feel aligned with our values and our enthusiasm will drop.

Time and time again, people circle back to me for help, but they are only willing to discuss values integration at an intellectual level and ignore the opportunity to use the heart and body centers to assess the values gaps and identify deeper changes that would truly bring the values to life. We expect that by simply telling people to uphold our new values, the change work has been done as leaders. This rarely works in other change initiatives, but for some reason, we stick to the same approach for something as deeply personal as values integration work.

An added issue that exists for some is the dissonance they feel when confronted with the gap between the desired values and their work realities. For example, they may feel stress levels when they're being asked to lie to a customer about supply chain issues after receiving the recent message about "our value of accountability." It's uncomfortable. And it creates huge amounts of distrust that spills into all the other areas of their work. They bring that tension and dissonance home and further amplify it by pretending to their family that they're fine, or they end up trying to release the built-up stress responses in a fight with their family.

When we avoid vulnerability because it's too uncomfortable or we believe it's wrong, we don't know how to talk about these disconnects—and it's crushing us.

We're becoming increasingly disconnected; we're losing tolerance, patience, empathy, and compassion for each other. There's no quick fix to this problem, but we can't give up. If our leadership expectations evolved to developing all our centers of intelligence, our self-awareness would expand tremendously. Vulnerability would be less intimidating, and we could slowly remove our metaphorical masks.

Let's explore this further in the next chapter.

REFLECTIONS ON YOUR EVOLVED LEADERSHIP JOURNEY

1. What beliefs about vulnerability might be impacting your leadership effectiveness?

2. Think of the best manager you've ever had. How did vulnerability show up in your relationship with them?

3. Where have you avoided tension in order to make the situation easier for yourself or others? Where would stepping more deeply into tension change the potential outcome for the better?

CHAPTER 7

THE NEVER-ENDING PRESSURE TO PERFORM

"Remember that time is money."

Benjamin Franklin, 1748[1]

For as long as I can remember, I've had an insatiable desire to learn new things. I recall as a young child telling my mom that I wanted to be the smartest person in the world. You might think that would translate into straight As or a Mensa membership, but it didn't. I wasn't even an honors student in high school or university. However, I was blessed with a learning style that allowed me to do reasonably well without studying too much. Unfortunately, history wasn't something I found interesting—it felt like a mechanical regurgitation of facts with little context. It wasn't until I was in my twenties that I started to grasp how relevant history is to our understanding of current political, economic, and social systems, all of which impact our workplaces.

This history lesson I wish I'd learned was that our obsession with productivity and efficiency is far from new. Franklin's quote was advice to the "young tradesman" of the day to be cautious of laziness if they wanted to be successful. Working longer hours meant more money. I think we could call Benjamin Franklin a workaholic, and his views were quite influential at the time. He retired at age forty-two from a successful printing business only to dive into other pursuits like science and politics.[2]

When the Industrial Revolution unfolded shortly thereafter in the 1760s, it catapulted productivity to new levels with the advent of the steam engine and power loom. All great things, right? Unfortunately, my high school history lessons never taught me about the pollution, public health challenges, child labor, or poor working conditions that came along with these advancements. Did you know it was common for workers to average fourteen-hour days, six days a week?[3]

Technological progress moved us through three more industrial revolutions after that, each one advancing our abilities to produce and manufacture better products at faster speeds while also allowing the original issues to proliferate. More output meant more revenue. More working hours meant even more revenue. How enticing for the wealthy leaders of these companies.

We are repeating the past. Our obsession for efficiency and productivity, like those before us, has continued to raise expectations of work performance, as if our human capabilities can keep up with the advancing automation.

It can't. And yet we keep trying.

We're wedged into a system, unable to find a way out.

I've always been driven to succeed, perhaps from my years of competitive sports and white privilege that have conditioned me to believe that winning happens with hard work and talent. As I grew older, I felt compelled to be the best employee, manager, wife, and mother. If I could perform without dropping any balls or without reproach, I could get promoted into bigger roles and assume broader and more complex responsibilities.

I never would have called myself a perfectionist. Did I have high standards? Yes, I did. It was part of being a high performer. Even through Paul's illness and raising the boys, I was challenging myself with new roles, getting promotions, and trying to develop as a leader. That's what you do when you have high standards, or so I thought.

What I didn't realize is that my strong desire to perform involved avoiding resistance from others by trying to please them. In my mind, that was the mark of an excellent employee: if you could foresee all challenges and be well prepared, then no question could go unanswered.

Discomfort stops us from pursuing the deeper, difficult moments in our lives: acknowledging that we don't know how to do something, or accepting that we're at fault; questioning whether the standard approach is always the right path to take or whether a policy should always be followed; trying something new when we might fail; standing up to bullying behavior from managers; saying no when we're already collapsing under our current workload.

Perfectionism is a nasty thing. I didn't know how deep its tentacles were wrapped around me. Even as I built my own business. I would continue to find myself avoiding hard conversations with clients about the work I really wanted to do with them because I was afraid they wouldn't rehire me. If I'm being honest, I even worried about people thinking I wasn't being a good widow. That's how destructive perfectionism is.

Productivity and perfectionism feed off each other. We get stuck in a cycle of chasing unattainable expectations but not giving up because we don't want to be blamed or judged.

It's a vicious cycle, and it's playing out every day in our workplaces. As we've discussed, we try to pretend that we were fine, but pretending that everything is fine can come at a cost.

GUARDING AGAINST SHOWING UP AS OUR REAL SELVES

The pandemic lockdown restrictions where I live were pretty strict. We spent a lot of time in our house, and it became very comfortable to live and work in the same place. As restrictions were lifted, some people couldn't get enough activity, while others preferred to stay home, even when no longer required. Either way, the sensory overload of coming back out into the world happened to all of us. I was so excited about returning to live concerts that I booked tickets to several big shows in the same month. We had been physically and socially deconditioned and were now unsure how to handle ourselves when we saw each other for the first time in real life. Would we fist bump?

Hug? Remember how to make small talk?

The CTRI notes, "[w]hat happens to one individual will affect how they relate to others, and how others relate to them. In this way, trauma is not just an individual experience. It even affects whole organizations by impacting the ways in which we do our work, serve our clients, and achieve our missions."[4]

Think about the last time you worked somewhere that had mass layoffs that seemed to affect everyone, even those employees who weren't part of the group who were let go or whether they knew any of the people who had lost their job. You carry the impact of that event with you, despite whether you can articulate why it has changed you. As a manager who experienced several right-sizings, I learned about the survivor's guilt felt by the people who weren't laid off and were unclear as to why they avoided a similar fate. For some people, their body might interpret these events as a new perceived threat.

Do you think of yourself as being vigilant in your job? I did. I examined what being vigilant meant: to keep a careful watch—a careful watch to make sure bad things don't happen; to avoid risk. When I reflect upon my own experience, the more responsibility I assumed in a role, the more vigilant I had to be. You want to be seen by your manager as being a diligent employee, and since you're getting paid for your performance, you can easily step into a state of hypervigilance.

So what does this do to our nervous systems? It puts us on high alert when we don't learn how to pull out of this vigilant state. It really impacts our body, especially if we have a past or present trauma, whether it stems from situational, racialized, or collective sources.

This constant state of hypervigilance tells our body to be on guard because of the perception of constant threats.

Couple hypervigilance with perfectionism and you've got a destructive combination that leads directly to burnout. Have you been there? Me too.

This is why vulnerability is essential to lead in today's world. As we've discussed, vulnerability is not about opening yourself up to be hurt. It's about leading with openness while holding yourself and others accountable. That means having uncomfortable conversations that are respectful and allow each party to be heard and accepted for their perspective. Ultimately, when leaders demonstrate vulnerability, it creates a feeling of belonging for the team.

Sometimes we want to deny that we have emotions because emotions aren't rewarded, and they aren't logical. We want to focus on tangible, "controllable" elements like productivity, work performance, or problem solving. We try to believe that we don't want to be vulnerable.

I used to think that vulnerability was only related to emotions like shame, fear, scarcity, and anxiety, and no one wants to feel that way. But I learned that vulnerability includes love, belonging, and joy. There are two ends to the vulnerability spectrum, and they are both uncomfortable because they are uncertain.

I used to cringe at the word *love*. It made me feel uneasy, and there was certainly no room for love at work. In speaking about his book *Love and Work*, Marcus Buckingham writes "you don't have to love all you do, but if you have a working situation where there's no love in it, you won't be creative. You won't innovate. You won't be resilient. All the outcomes that we want, you won't get without love."[5] Still, love at work is a hard sell. But belonging at work? That's much more palatable and it's taken a huge leap forward in importance for CEOs. Deloitte's 2020 Human Capital Trends report showed that 79 percent of organizations said that fostering a sense of belonging in the workforce was important to their organization's success in the next 12–18 months, and 93 percent agreed that a sense of belonging drives organizational performance—one of the highest rates of consensus on importance they have seen in a decade of Global Human Capital Trends reports.[6]

If we're going to truly create places where people feel like they belong, then vulnerability has to happen.

When we don't feel we can be our true selves at work and acknowledge the messiness or struggles we're feeling, we manage them by using self-protective behaviors, or practice "armoring up" as Brené Brown calls it.[7] We push down our feelings, slap smiles on our faces, and tell everyone we're fine.

Sometimes we cope by overworking, numbing, or using sarcasm to get us through and mask how we're feeling or whether we're struggling. I've seen guarded behavior occur in repeatable patterns across the hundreds of people I've trained and coached in the past fifteen years, and in myself.

As we come out of the urgency phase of the pandemic, we're trying to return to the way things used to be while avoiding the discomfort of facing some hard truths that are polarizing and divisive—truths that our social systems are decimated, that our racial ignorance has existed for far too long, and that wars will never stop. And the truth is that we can't return to the way things used to be—at home or at work. As leaders, we have to learn how to manage polarities without trying to find the right answer or fix it.

HOW TRAUMA LEADS TO GUARDED BEHAVIOR

We're carrying trauma from the pandemic into our daily work lives, leaving us watchful and worried. If we're unsure whether the dangers that can affect us have been averted, we're keeping our nervous system on high alert. If we had someone at work who could reassure us, we might de-escalate. As Burke Harris notes in *The Deepest Well*, "the key to keeping a tolerable stress response from tipping over into the toxic stress zone is the presence of a buffering adult to adequately mitigate the impact of the stressor."[8] Since we're all in the same boat, trying to navigate this new reality without certainties or best practices to guide us, we're operating without others around us to reassure us about what to do next.

We're looking for safety, and it's getting harder to find. We're operating at such a fast pace, in so much uncertainty, and we're dragging along some old practices that are believed to drive performance and keep productivity levels high.

One of the most toxic and destructive workplace practices is the performance review, the time once or twice a year when your manager evaluates your performance and tells you what kind of value you bring as an employee. It's often a lopsided perspective, usually based on a few data points that the manager deems true. It's a broken process that keeps people in a state of constant hypervigilance. According to Gallup, only 14 percent of employees strongly agree their performance reviews help by inspiring them to improve.[9]

We cram these reviews into our busy agendas. And try as we like, it's very hard to be present and create a safe space because many times we are forced to put people into a bell curve. We usually don't have control over how much money is going to be given, and as leaders, we're forced into a situation where we want to honor the employee for their hard work and dedication but have no control or very little control over remuneration because there's a bigger system at play.

Performance reviews have an inherent power dynamic that can wreak havoc on our nervous system. What if leaders and their teams co-created a system for how to measure their performance? It's vulnerable, that's for sure. Maybe it would be a combination of individual performance and meeting team objectives? There's no singular approach that will work for everyone, but something has to change.

Why have we created a system to handle the (typically) few slackers? Instead, why can't we create a system that serves the most?

Are these people really slackers? Maybe. More often, though, those perceived slackers are unclear on expectations and aren't sure how to talk about it. Both parties then avoid the discomfort of having a vulnerable conversation and provide a multitude of excuses ranging from "I don't have time right now" to "they should just know." The performance gap widens, and everyone is frustrated. Ultimately, the manager needs to take the lead and make these conversations a priority. Performance management requires conversations on a regular basis.

SEVEN PROFILES OF GUARDED BEHAVIOR AT WORK

There are typical modes of working that people rely on to avoid dealing with their stress and its side effects, including numbing or detaching from thinking deeply about the issues they're facing. We're trying to "fake it till we make it" where we shield ourselves from being vulnerable by pretending to be authentic and tell others that we're fine while adding protective actions to keep us from dealing with the fear.

As you'll see from the descriptions, each of these profiles—I call them archetypes in my workshops—are rewarded in some way, so we keep doing them. And the cycle continues.

There are things that we do to avoid the discomfort of being wrong, being overwhelmed, or losing control. They show up every day in all our workplaces. You might identify with one of them, or possibly a few, or even more than that. I can tell you that I've been all these people at different points in my career.

This is what running from discomfort can look like and the different ways that we try to control the situation and protect ourselves from uncertainty. For many of us, they are instinctual responses that don't seem problematic. These behaviors have been normalized and rewarded in our workplace because they serve our desire to be productive and efficient, but they are really all about protecting ourselves from true authenticity.

The importance of understanding these archetypes is that it will help you identify when and why you might be resorting to protective behavior. Maybe you already know. With this insight, you gain the agency to choose your response with intention. Perhaps it's an authoritative boss who won't take no for an answer. Perhaps it's an automatic reaction you weren't aware of. Either way, it's unknowingly preventing you from living to your full potential.

It's not realistic to stop these behaviors completely. It is about learning discernment with them so you can intentionally choose when it's safe to let your authenticity shine. And when your self-awareness evolves, it brings in more self-compassion for you and the people you work with.

The Seven Guarded Archetypes include:

1. The Dominant Doer
2. The Misguided Multitasker
3. The Yes Yeller
4. The Abdicating Apologizer
5. The Vocal Volunteer
6. The Abundant Asker
7. The Perpetual Procrastinator

Let's look at these profiles in more detail.

1) THE DOMINANT DOER.

"I'm on it."

I used to pride myself on the fact that you would always receive a reply from me within thirty minutes. This included emails, texts, IMs, and calls. You name it, I was ready at your service to please and perform. I didn't ever want you to worry that you weren't heard or being looked after.

Signs of a Dominant Doer:

- Powering through the day without taking breaks (not even bathroom or lunch breaks)
- Dropping hobbies to work late because there's too much to do
- Realizing in mid-November that you still have six weeks of banked vacation and can't possibly use all the days
- Replying to emails despite being away and having an "out of office" notification because you believe it's better to take a few minutes now to avoid a mountain of messages later

When this happens, you are defining your self-worth by how productive you appear to be. It's driven from a place of pleasing others and being available to get things done. These behaviors are highly valued in organizations and many people tout themselves as being "highly productive."

2) THE MISGUIDED MULTITASKER.

"Just need one more minute."

Productivity is like a drug. You get a "zing" when checking off the items on your list or even adding a task you've completed so you can enjoy crossing it off. It's a dopamine hit, a neurochemical that makes you feel good, especially if you can check off a few at the same time. It can also look like trying to cram an unreasonable amount of work into the available time you have.

Signs of a Misguided Multitasker:

- Answering emails while you're on the phone and can't be seen by the caller
- Checking texts while someone is speaking to you; you might even say, "don't worry, I'm still listening"
- Doing "light tasks" while watching a movie with your kids or bringing your laptop to bed when spending "quality time" with your partner
- Working on several projects at once, using multiple screens

You're doing a lot of things because there's a sense of scarcity—not enough time, money, or resources. There's just a sense of "not enough." When this happens, you're avoiding accepting that you can't do it all, and like the Dominant Doer, you're taking on more than you can do to avoid having to say no to the people who are asking more of you.

3) THE YES YELLER.

"Sure thing. I'll do it!"

We all know this person (especially if we are this person). Leaders rely on the people who always say yes because they are dependable and continuously get things done. "No" is not in their vocabulary for fear that it might upset someone. It's simply easier to say yes now and figure it out later, because at no cost will they disappoint someone.

Signs of a Yes Yeller:

- Not considering your existing workload or deadlines when accepting new assignments
- Disappointing family members by being late or skipping previous commitments because of work
- Extending the hours of your workday to get "one more thing" done
- Taking over tasks from others because they are struggling and it will be faster if you do them

What's happening here? Ultimately, this is about avoiding tough conversations for fear of upsetting others. Boundaries are loose or nonexistent as we try to remain flexible and ensure the needs of others are accommodated first.

4) THE ABDICATING APOLOGIZER.

"Sorry about that. So sorry."

I hear "sorry" a lot, which might be because I live in Canada, but there's a universal truth to it. In the corporate world, people are apologizing for things they don't need to, often without even realizing it.

Signs of an Abdicating Apologizer:

- Apologizing for something that might happen in the future: "Sorry if that causes issues for you."
- Accepting more than your share of responsibility for an issue: "I should have known better."
- Starting off a meeting with "Sorry I'm late, my other meeting went long."
- Beginning an email with "Sorry I didn't get back to you sooner" or "I just have a quick question."

What's happening here? At the root of this behavior is the fact that if I look and act perfectly, you can't judge me or tell me I'm wrong. So I'll beat you to it by apologizing and acknowledging my imperfection before you can tell me. Words like *just* and *should* will also show up here and take away your power. Statements like "thanks for your patience" or "your expertise would be really helpful" are more suitable responses.

5) THE VOCAL VOLUNTEER.

"Of course I can help! What do you need?"

This person is everywhere, and you can always count on them to give their time. They volunteer for committees and stay after hours to help with a project—they insert themselves into every possible opportunity. They're like the Energizer Bunny that never stops. They take the minutes, send out the invites, and (seem to) have their hand up to volunteer at every possible instance.

Signs of a Vocal Volunteer:

- Signing up for responsibilities outside of normal office hours
- Asking for more assignments, even if they're at or over capacity
- Always being the one to take minutes at meetings
- Being at the center of every single company social event

What's happening here? Sometimes mistaken as being overly generous or seen as a committed employee, this person is really hustling to show their value. This behavior looks like the Yes Yeller, but their motivation is different. They're not entirely sure what people value in them, so they're everywhere. The common response for this type of behavior is "they're so committed" or "we can always count on them." Yes you can, but at what expense?

6) THE ABUNDANT ASKER.

"Is it okay if I send it to you first to have a look?"

Being curious and asking questions are important qualities, but they are sometimes used to deflect fear and sidestep accountability. However, our hierarchical structures drive more asking-for-permission behaviors (a.k.a. "covering your a**" mantras in many companies) than genuine curiosity.

Signs of an Abundant Asker:

- Seeking input or approval for decisions within their control
- Defaulting to others in meetings without stating their perspective
- Answering their manager's question with "I'm not sure, what do you think?"
- Having to check with their boss first to make sure they're not missing anything

This is a vicious cycle that gets perpetuated by managers afraid of being wrong and losing control. They inadvertently demonstrate that correct answers are valued more than learning from mistakes. They end up answering simple questions because it's faster than pausing, inquiring, and coaching in the moment. When left unbroken, both parties are frustrated, and trust is impacted. Managers think they can't trust their team to do the right thing and fester about why their teams can't make decisions on their own.

7) THE PERPETUAL PROCRASTINATOR.

"I'm going to need more time."

The common theory used to be that procrastination was a sign of laziness. Perhaps you still believe that. However, procrastination is much more about numbing out emotions and finding another activity with which to distract yourself. Surfing the internet, scrolling through social media, and binge-watching shows can all be signs of avoiding a particular task.

Signs of a Perpetual Procrastinator:

- Not following extensive work plans
- Poorly estimating the time needed for task completion
- Continually asking for timeline extensions
- Sharing a multitude of reasons to explain why a task isn't completed

What's happening here? It's not that you're lazy; it could mean you have feelings of inadequacy and self-doubt. There's a time to relax but that's very different from procrastinating. I used to say that I was good under pressure and better at leaving things until the last minute. What I realize now is that I was so consumed with doing it the "right way" that I would put it off until the pressure was so great that I had no other choice but to complete it.

I know it can be confronting to see these guarded behaviors all at once. Did you recognize yourself in any of them? These are ways we self-protect and hide. And the impact? It keeps us from being able to connect deeply to our work and to each other. Our values, and the ones our companies try to get us to buy into, get compromised because they require vulnerability—and we can't be vulnerable when we're trying to protect ourselves.

How do we shift the narrative?

WHEN GUARDED BEHAVIOR CAN BECOME UNLOCKED

With age, I've been able to let go of my quest for perfection. I still work at a high intensity, so I don't always get this right, but I'm not as caught up in productivity and perfection performances.

Part of it started for me in setting new boundaries for the standards I wanted to uphold, not just absorbing the often unrealistic expectations set by others. Evolving my awareness of these patterns has been life changing. I've been able to loosen the grips of ego and personality so that a deeper authenticity emerges. It's what inspired me to be a Human Spirit Ignitor and ignite others to evolve their leadership.

Let's dive into that in the next chapter.

REFLECTIONS ON YOUR EVOLVED LEADERSHIP JOURNEY

1. What does productivity mean to you and how does it influence your leadership?

2. Which of the seven profiles do you exhibit? Observe yourself one day and see if your observations matched your response.

3. What is the most common behavior from the seven profiles that you see in your team or direct reports? How might you help reduce the prevalence of it?

CHAPTER 8

BECOMING AN EVOLVED LEADER

"'Leadership' is wanting to do something new and better, and getting others to go along."

–Edgar H. Schein[1]

Facilitating meetings has always been something I love doing, especially with a formal leadership title. I could use that positional power for good and ensure all voices were given the time they deserved. Several years ago, I was leading a meeting with my team. We had a lot to get through, including making an important decision by consensus. It was a contentious topic, but I was confident we would find alignment. I left the meeting feeling great—everyone had shared their thoughts, and we agreed on a way forward. I was settling into the chair in my office, silently praising myself for facilitating a kick-ass meeting and deftly inviting all voices, when one of my direct reports knocked on the door and had a concerned look on her face. I invited her in and asked if there was anything wrong. She said, “Next time you have your mind made up like that don’t pretend to care about what we think.”

The feeling of that moment has never left me. The gap between my desired intention and actual impact was vast, far greater than I could have imagined. That’s when I learned that self-awareness is a journey, not a destination.

There will always be a mix of behaviors we don’t see and ones we’re consciously trying to change. This is true regardless of where you are in your leadership journey. Just when you think you’ve got it figured out is precisely the moment you should be looking further inward at yourself.

Self-awareness has been acknowledged as a key differentiator in leadership, contributing to individual effectiveness and correlated with corporate performance.[2] However, it’s often overlooked on development plans or seen as taking too much time for leaders to invest into making.

It’s nonnegotiable now. Self-awareness is the foundation for the evolved leader. It frames the path forward to loosen the power of the ego, giving one access to their authentic being.

Let’s look at how we can evolve into a new mode of leading.

AUTHENTIC LEADERSHIP 2.0

In 2018, I completed my master’s degree in industrial and organizational psychology, and I focused my thesis on authentic leadership.

I was looking for the foundations of leadership that could contribute to a great employee experience. I built a model called Purposeful Workplace Experiences™ (PWE), and it consisted of four synergistic elements essential for a healthy culture: connection, collaboration, adaptability, equivalence.

PWE encouraged leaders to focus on designing a work environment, one that would make employees less stressed and more productive. This was a design-thinking approach built on looking at the organization through the lens of employees to see how they were impacted by factors such as work environment, relational interactions, and performance processes.

THE PURPOSEFUL WORKPLACE EXPERIENCE

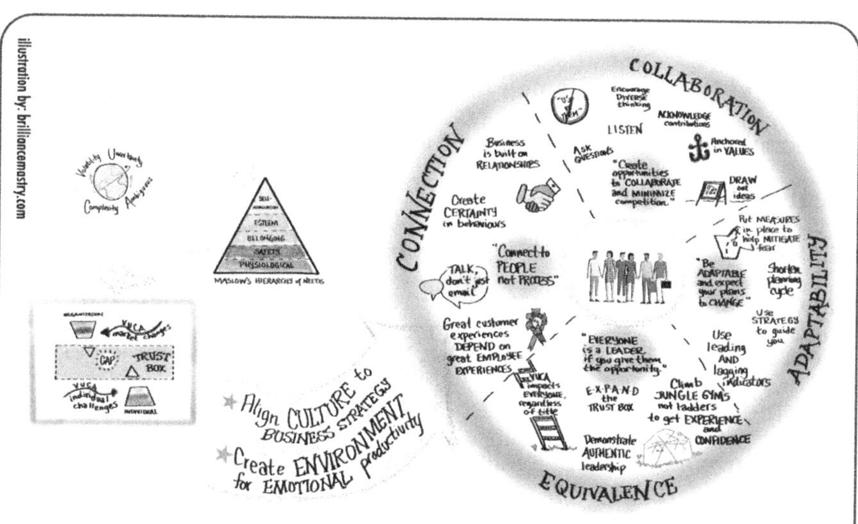

Interested in increasing productivity and reducing employee turnover? Let go of outdated models of thinking that treat organizations and people like machines. The business climate is unpredictable, volatile, and complex, making it essential to consciously shape your workplace culture at all times. The Purposeful Workspace Experience is your best defense. It creates a workplace that helps drive alignment between an individual and their organization. It increases engagement, improves productivity, and elevates creativity by focusing on human needs first. The workplace is being disrupted, and we need to embrace new ways of working. We need to evolve, and the Purposeful Workplace Experience is an essential part of breaking out of old organizational patterns.

It was the basis of my first book, *Rules of Engagement*. I was determined to help leaders create work environments that felt connected to a bigger purpose—something employees would see as part of their experiences too. I had witnessed the increase in excitement when people could connect their work to a purpose that mattered to them. This translated into increased momentum and ultimately, financial success.

While the book did reasonably well in sales, over the years the concepts of PWE weren't translating to lasting change with clients. Yet another lesson in learning that good intention doesn't always lead to the impact you're hoping for.

Upon reflection, what was missing from that work was a focus on the leader themselves. My additional training and certifications since writing that book validated this fact as well. Now I see the PWE as the vision and trauma-informed leadership as how you get there.

Too often people get moved into leadership roles and aren't provided adequate leadership training or support with the transition. They are expected to thrive, even though the technical skills that helped them stand out are rarely what's needed to be a successful leader. We expect leaders to be genuine and authentic, but we forget that their experience as employees needs to be part of the equation as well.

The concept of servant leadership, which was developed in the 1970s by Robert Greenleaf, a director of research at AT&T, was discussed in boardrooms in the 1990s and 2000s. Despite its religious overtones, the idea that managers should be selfless and committed to their employees was popular, even though it ignored the power dynamics that leaders held over their teams. It wasn't the answer.

Using the word *authenticity* with *leadership* has been studied for decades. Early research stated that authentic leadership theory was leaders inspiring others through values and setting an example through what they do.[3] When Bill George, former CEO of Medtronic, published his book *Authentic Leadership*, it amplified the importance of leading with an ethical purpose and being grounded in strong personal values.

One could argue that being authentic might mean responding to whatever emotions bubble up in difficult team meetings or being okay with being blunt and harsh in performance-development conversations. From the conversations I've had with people over the years, there are a number of leaders who are applying this literal definition of authenticity, but it's only ego-centric behavior trying to force performance out of people.

Let me be clear that this is not authenticity. When leaders are authentic, it positively influences employee reactions by setting an organization's psychological climate by creating predictable and stable behaviors.[4] Dumping intense emotions onto others is fear-based behavior that is reactive and driven by ego. It's a resistance to vulnerability, and when people in leadership positions act like this, even if it's not all the time, it creates instability in the working relationship. Trust is eroded because there is no certainty in how they will act. It becomes safer to respond with the protective behaviors we talked about in Chapter 7.

Coaching managers and senior leaders has been part of my consulting practice for many years, and before starting my own business, coaching had always been part of my corporate jobs. When coaching someone, and then meeting them later in a group setting, I could see at times how different they seemed. In our one-to-one sessions, they were open, candid, and honest. They would share some of their deepest fears and challenges, and we would talk through them together to help shape next steps. Yet days or weeks or even hours later, they would revert to using the overly confident bravado that they felt was the appropriate way for leaders to behave.

The question at the core of my curiosity about authentic leadership was this: Why are executives or other senior leaders different in one-to-one settings than they are in groups? Why can't leaders be their true selves in every setting, not just when they're alone with someone they feel is safe enough to open up to?

INTEGRATING YOUR CENTERS OF INTELLIGENCE

In Chapter 3, we learned about the head, heart, and body centers of intelligence. When they are integrated and balanced, we are able to think objectively, build relationships, and swiftly take the right action.

Our self-awareness journey involves getting familiar with these centers, understanding which one is most dominant for us, and then learning how it influences our thinking and feeling patterns. This leads to integration and balance, which means we are able to use the appropriate center when needed and not try to problem solve exclusively with our emotions or build strategic plans on the impulse of our bodies. The more balance we can find in using these centers, the more we are able to expand our authentic interactions to larger groups.

BECOMING TRAUMA-INFORMED LEADERS

"All of us want to shine as brightly as we can. It's as if we come into this world bearing spark, one that longs to be fanned into a flame of authentic selfhood. There is nothing inherently domineering about that pure desire to shine, nothing in it that must suck up all the oxygen and extinguish other flames. There's a way to reveal one's singing self without diminishing the light of another."

–Elizabeth Lesser, *Cassandra Speaks*[5]

When we add the awareness of using our centers of intelligence and an understanding of trauma, it changes our expectations of leaders. Once we acknowledge that everyone we encounter has survived some amount of trauma, ranging from small-t trauma to big-T trauma, it helps us understand that a new mode of leadership is needed—one that helps us show up in a way that will bring a tone of safety to the people we encounter. We don't need to know what kind of trauma they face, or to what degree. It's our job to lead in a way that reflects a calm nervous system and sets expectations for psychological safety.

Evolved leaders who are trauma-informed are able to lean into the vulnerability and release the need for control. As Elizabeth Lesser notes in *Cassandra Speaks*, we need to move away from celebrating the values of domination and control and begin embracing the values of care and belonging. We need to balance values of accountability and integrity equally with openness, empathy, compassion, and communication.[6]

We want to create a "mindful presence" where we lead with intention, self-control, and a broad awareness and understanding of our own needs and the needs of our team. Author Rick Hanson refers to presence as a mindful state of awareness that keeps us grounded and connected to the present moment.[7] It's not easy to do, but it's exactly what's needed in today's complex and uncertain dynamic.

What's at the core of Evolved Leadership is acknowledging that the way you've been successful up until now has been by operating largely in protection mode. This echoes the research findings from Gartner shared in Chapter 2 that less than a third of employees feel their leaders are authentic.[8] Understanding that your behaviors come from past stress or trauma and have informed how you operate day to day, and seeing how the same is true for the people you lead, becomes the step to unlocking a new way of being as a leader. It brings compassion and kindness to the forefront but not at the expense of performance.

As you work through understanding and managing how you show up at work, you'll increase your resilience and broaden your window of tolerance. And as you do this work, you'll notice a similar settling and expanded resilience from your team. You'll set a tone of safety, trust, and openness that will signal to others that it's safe to work with you.

Now, what each of us deems to be a crisis or needs to feel safe is going to be different based on our history, experience, or race. Being trauma-informed isn't going to require us to understand all those details or unpack any of them. Being trauma-informed is about recognizing how to keep our nervous systems calm and reduce the need for hypervigilance.

You'll notice that being trauma-informed means you and your team will be able to navigate the uncertainties and complexities of your work post-pandemic without inducing a massive stress response. Remember, though, as we continue to dive into the work of an evolved leader, being trauma-informed does not mean you need to identify or fix someone else's trauma. That's not your role. Your role is to be consistent in your behaviors and set expectations for safe team interactions. I've seen many leaders do the following:

- Recognize when they are in a reactive state and instead of dumping their emotions impulsively, they step away and circle back. It might be a few minutes or a day.
- Establish guidelines for participation at meetings without assuming everyone should know what they are and collectively acknowledge them to start all meetings. For example, cameras on for virtual meetings or excuse yourself from the room if you need to use your phone.
- Co-create a brave space together by listing what people need to be able to show up fully. This is especially helpful for longer meetings and/or topics with wide-ranging opinions.

- Do a check-in round with everyone in the room to start a meeting. It can be "one word to describe how you're feeling" or "your intention for this meeting."

FINDING SELF-COMPASSION

The more we learn about ourselves, the more we see how imperfect we truly are. It is in this imperfection where your authenticity lies. You can't reach this part of yourself without deep self-compassion. It is your partner on this journey that you cannot live without. It will remind you that you're not alone, it will teach you how to say gentle words to yourself, and it will help you move through emotions instead of getting stuck in them.

A friendly reminder that self-compassion does not equate to a lack of accountability. Instead, it's a kind voice that balances the inner critic who can take over our thoughts and demand performance at all costs. And the amazing thing about compassion is that the more you give yourself, the more you can give others. David Rock notes, "compassion doesn't just help us be patient with ourselves; it also increases our ability to be patient with others who may also be struggling."[9]

Leadership is really about finding your true authentic self because that's when you are the most believable, the most open, and the most successful. Let's get practical now and explore three principles of Evolved Leadership, grounded in your authenticity, not your ego.

REFLECTIONS ON YOUR EVOLVED LEADERSHIP JOURNEY

1. Recall a leadership situation when you were shocked to learn that the impact of your actions was drastically different than your intention. What lesson did that teach you?

2. Who are the people that you are most authentic with at work? Peers, direct reports, managers? What might this be telling you?

3. How compassionate are you really with yourself? Check out this assessment to explore areas that can help you tap into more compassion. https://self-compassion.org/self-compassion-test/

CHAPTER 9

THREE PRINCIPLES FOR EVOLVED LEADERS

It sounds terrible to say, but the isolation brought on by the pandemic was a blessing for me. Overnight, like millions of other people around the world, I stopped traveling, and all my workshop delivery switched to online formats. Even my proposal pitch meetings and coaching happened on virtual platforms.

I was fortunate that my work largely continued as usual; I know this is not the case for others. The end of travel and commuting created new space in my calendar. Instead of waking up every morning and dashing out the door, I had time to sit, eat breakfast, read, and reflect before my day started. The changing environment for my business and personal life forced me to slow down and created the conditions aligned for me to do deep personal work. I know it's a privileged position to look at the circumstances of the pandemic in this way, and I know many people had an incredibly difficult time.

I started to look back at the key points in my life that were challenging and began figuring out how to make sense of them. I pieced together the story of my life, uncovered new insights, faced hard realities, and unraveled elements of my personality that made me mentally and emotionally exhausted. I've found a new language to make meaning of things, and this healing has opened me up in profound ways.

The biggest surprise during this time was realizing the impact of being imbalanced in my centers of intelligence and how much I had suppressed my emotions, especially grief. There was the obvious grief related to Paul's death but also buried feelings about my dad's death and our entire relationship. His passing came quickly: only a few weeks after a cancer diagnosis and three weeks before Paul's death.

At the same time, the pandemic was eliciting strong feelings for people, and they were defining their new feelings as potentially grief.[1] In workshops, I even heard a few people say they felt traumatized by their experiences with leaders at that time. This was followed by plenty of client work to create spaces for employees to open up and share, to intentionally connect and check in on each other. As the lockdown extended from weeks to months, these sessions slowed down and teams returned to their focus on the business, trying to adapt to virtual meetings and asynchronous working methods.

But I could see signs of sadness re-emerging as people worked virtually or risked their safety by going into their workplace. What was happening? When I came across the work of Pauline Boss and her research in ambiguous loss, it helped fill in some gaps. She states in her book *The Myth of Closure*, "It's understandable to feel weary and sad after what many experienced during the pandemic and its fellow stressors—racism, politics, poverty, food shortages, loss of income, family violence, suicides, and home-grown terrorism. Surely, there will be no closure on the mountain of losses caused by the pandemic, but now, we must try to find meaning in them. Perhaps that meaning lies in working for change."[2]

Find meaning in all of this—that's something leaders can do but it does require one to look inward. It's a big ask, especially among so many other responsibilities leaders carry. It's hard to know what leadership skills would work best to support it. When we consider the different scenarios, time horizons, and differing levels of complexity and uncertainty leaders need to navigate through, you might wonder if leaders should have one operating style for day-to-day business and another for significant change programs. Like the leadership equivalent of having both a suit and business-casual clothes for Fridays. And since we know now that being connected to our three centers of intelligence as well as understanding the changes that our individual and shared traumas have created, does this mean there's yet another set of skills leaders need to learn?

You'll be happy to hear that my answer is no. There's one set of skills that leaders need in every work scenario—whether in times of relative calm or in the height of chaos. We talked about it earlier: safety, consistency, and authenticity. This is the path to being an evolved leader, to authenticity, and to creating an environment that feels inspiring and challenging yet safe and accepting.

When I think about all the different leadership roles I've had and all the leaders I've had the privilege to work with in my career, what employees in all those scenarios craved was certainty. And if they couldn't have certainty of outcomes, they at least wanted to be able to trust that their leader was going to act in a consistent, reliable, steady way to guide the team to the right solutions. And this is exactly what leaders need to be doing now.

Let's look at how to create this for your teams.

CALM AND STEADY: THE EVOLVED LEADER MODEL

Today's workforce needs a leader who is a calm presence for their team, one who understands and stays connected to their people and their needs while remaining flexible to the changing needs of their work. The pandemic has shown us that all the planning in the world can't cover every scenario. Staying open and flexible to adapt to what's needed next is critical.

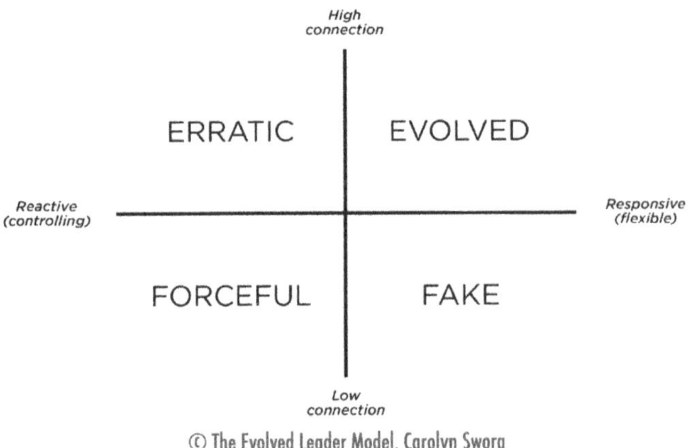

© The Evolved Leader Model, Carolyn Swora

The two variables that anchor the Evolved Leader Model are the basis for consistency, safety, and authenticity, as we discussed in Chapters 2 and 8. These variables, connection and reactivity, might surprise you, but it's how they combine that create the outcomes your teams need.

Connection (y-axis): This is the relational ability to stay in sync with the activities and mindset of your team members and colleagues, to guide them through any challenges or issues they encounter in their work. It's easy for us to be invisible at work, whether we're working in the office or working remotely; connection helps us feel more visible.

If you're low in connection, you could be focusing on tasks over relationships, productivity over people, and putting aside the feelings and reactions of others. When determining where you fall on this axis, consider where you go most often and during times of stress.

Reactivity (x-axis): This axis is about how we respond in our interactions with others. It ranges from an impulsive, unconscious reaction to a conscious, mindful response. There are underlying motivators that drive our behaviors, and the more conscious we are about them, the more flexible and less controlling we are. This is the ability to be responsive to changing needs from your environment, based on the physical, mental, and emotional needs of your team without enforcing your own agenda to control the outcome. This isn't changing your mind constantly, it's about being open to the need to course-correct or make adjustments as issues arise or new information is learned.

When you're highly reactive, others experience you as defensive or judgmental, and curiosity is hard to foster. When determining where you fall on this axis, think of how you respond when stakes are high and you have a meaningful attachment to the outcome.

The reality is we will find ourselves in each of these quadrants at some point, but the goal is to be consistently in the Evolve quadrant. Let's look at the combinations of connection and reactivity more closely:

When you're in the **Fake** zone, your strength is being **responsive** to the needs and insights of your team. You're perceived as flexible with less controlling behaviors, so people are less likely to feel judged. The challenge is that there is **low connection**. You don't have strong working relationships with the team. Perhaps you're new in the role or the team is geographically dispersed, or maybe you haven't made it a priority to build relationships with them. In this case, you can be perceived as lacking in consistency or reliability, leading to low trust.

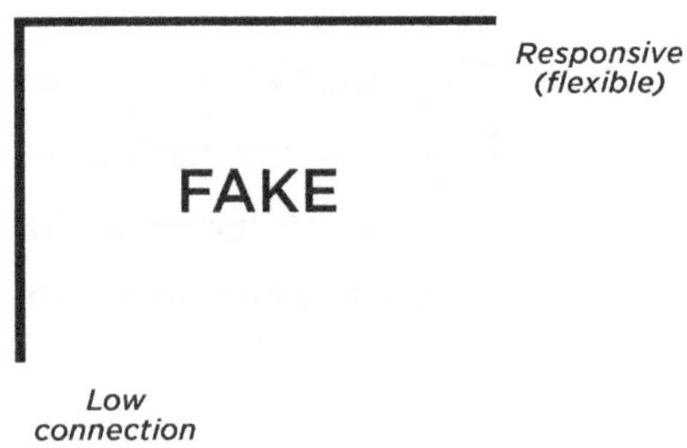

Example: In meetings, you invite insights from team members and can pivot in response to new ideas. However, you might be plowing through meeting agendas to ensure efficiency, or you might not be acknowledging contributions or validating the participation of others in the room.

Being in the **Forceful** zone means you're **highly reactive** with **low connection**. Leading from this place might lead to short-term results with a team, but it's not going to inspire the performance you need long term. When connection with others is compromised, people won't feel heard or seen, especially with impulsive reactions from you as their leader. You'll be seen as pushy and aggressive, leading to low trust on your team.

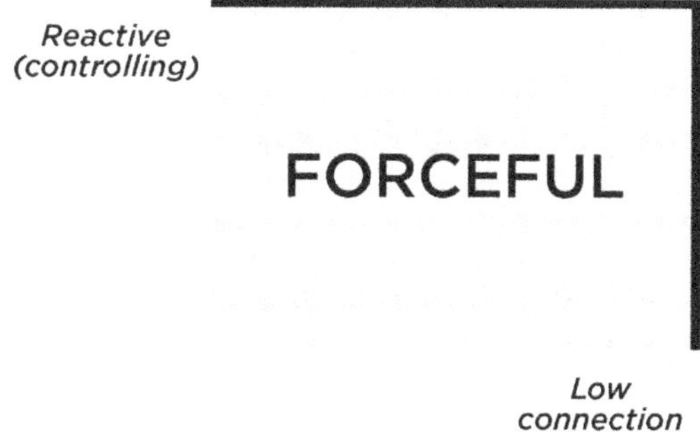

Example: A crisis has unfolded on your team, and you need to create an action plan immediately for the executive team to approve. You write out the plan yourself, tell the team this is what needs to be done, and suggest if anyone has additions to let you know as soon as possible.

The **Erratic** zone is where **high connection** is your strength. However, your relationships are negatively impacted by your **high reactivity** and impulsive tendencies. The team doesn't know what to expect. You overestimate the strength of relationships with your team, and they won't trust you because they know you're likely to react impulsively, often with controlling behaviors.

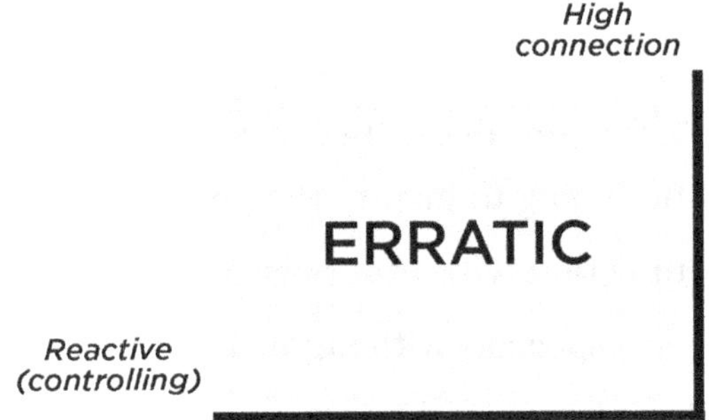

Example: You have meaningful one-to-one meetings and feel aligned. However, in larger group settings when there's broader discussion, you can get overwhelmed with all the input and be less consistent with decision-making and managing group discussions.

Being in the **Evolved** zone is the ideal place for leaders. There are **high levels of connection** with a high amount of conscious, **responsive** behaviors. Your team will feel an increased sense of safety and connection because they know you will work in concert with them, not in opposition. You can mindfully challenge thinking and inspire better performance. These factors lead to high trust, and in being energized by your work and through your actions, you help others feel energized in their work too.

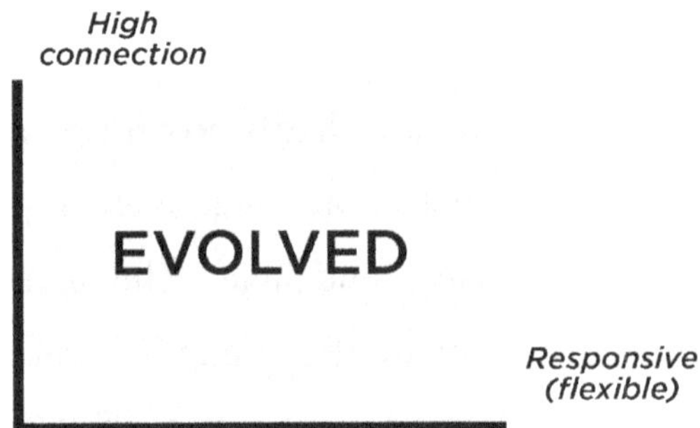

Example: A new product is being developed and the team has to make some important decisions in collaboration with another team. There are a few areas of contention, but you lead a meeting with everyone and create an agenda that allows full opportunity for everyone to contribute. You acknowledge contributions and get agreement from the team for the final decision.

Our intentions toward how we operate within these two axes need to be active and deliberate: we need to set out each day with the variables of connection and reactivity in mind.

There are three principles that can help us shift into the mindset of the Evolved Leader, ensuring that these principles come to life in our work and interactions with our team members:

1. **Self-Awareness (observing patterns of behavior)** – understanding what motives drive your behaviors, exploring biases, embracing feedback as a growth opportunity
2. **Self-Regulation (staying in control)** – being calm and mindful through the range of emotions and being conscious of situations that can trigger intense emotions (e.g., anger, shame) to actively anticipate how to avoid or minimize your own stress or trauma response
3. **Co-Regulation (managing your connection with others)** – entering every conversation or interaction with the intention of managing your self-control to avoid unnecessarily activating a stress or trauma response in others

Let's look at each of these principles more closely.

SELF-AWARENESS: OBSERVING PATTERNS OF BEHAVIOR

It's not an earth-shattering revelation that leaders need high levels of self-awareness to be successful, so I'm sure you aren't surprised to see it mentioned here.

My experience has been that leaders see this as a "point in time" exploration activity that has a start, middle, and end, believing that once new insights have been gleaned and a small number of changes have been attempted, we can check that box and move on.

Not so fast.

Self-awareness is a "forever and ever" activity—you will continue to have new challenges, opportunities, or initiatives requiring new solutions and skills. The key is getting curious about your unconscious behaviors, your biases, and your defense mechanisms so you can minimize the issues they create.

If you're skeptical about investing time into self-awareness, let me assure you that there is an abundance of research to prove its impact on leadership and performance. Psychologist Daniel Goleman highlights that strong self-awareness likely means you have strengths in other leadership areas as well.[3] Furthermore, the benefits of expanding your self-awareness go beyond you. Research from Korn Ferry shows 92 percent of leaders with high levels of self-awareness also have teams with high energy and high performance.[4]

Here are two practices that will evolve your self-awareness. While you can do them individually at separate times, you will find faster growth when you integrate them into a routine.

1. **Analysis from Insight Tools**

   Using self-assessment tools helps pinpoint strengths, areas needing attention, and ineffective patterns of behaviors. While it can be confronting, this knowledge is essential for

Evolved Leadership. These reports help identify where the gaps (large and small) of unintended impact might exist for you.

Certainly, there are self-assessment tools that can help you with the first path of self-awareness. I've used many of these in my work, including DiSC, Myers Briggs, Kolbe, SDI, and Leadership Circle, and there are hundreds of others, with varying levels of reliability and value.

In Chapter 3, we talked about the three centers of intelligence and their importance in evolving our leadership. The only tool that incorporates this concept is the Enneagram, which is why it is my preference. The Enneagram offers profound insight about what motivates us, the unconscious things that limit our self-awareness, and defense mechanisms that work hard to keep our ego in the driver's seat. Enneagram typing is based on core motivators, not behaviors. It dives deeper than what we do and gives us reason as to why we do it. And if that wasn't enough, another benefit of the Enneagram is its focus on growth pathways over simply knowing your own tendencies. Once you know your type, the Enneagram system lays out a path of development that addresses the motivator behind the behavior, hence addressing the root cause, not simply the surface issues.

One final note about the Enneagram. Discovering your type can be a powerful learning experience. I would encourage you to let your curiosity take the lead. Use reports or coaches to assist you, but you're the only one who truly can identify your Enneagram type.

2. **Perspective Sharing**
   Reaching out to trusted colleagues, customers, or others in the organization who interact with you regularly can give you lots of data for making changes or improvements. Inquire with questions like "What's your experience of me?" or "What works well in how we collaborate and what might be helpful for me to be more mindful of?"
   Our reactivity to feedback speaks volumes, so pay attention to it. Can you receive it with curiosity and openness? Maybe you smile and say thank you but deep down feel hurt or undervalued. Perhaps a defensive reply comes out because you're thinking they haven't known you long enough to know what you're really like.
   Feedback can elicit strong, visceral reactions because it's a reminder that we're not perfect. It takes conscious work to accept imperfection—that's why reactivity is part of the Evolved Leader Model.
   Seeking perspective from others needs to be done with a genuine interest in hearing observations from people who matter in your work and life. Years ago, I worked with a colleague to deliver a leadership workshop series. I admired her approach and was keen to learn new co-facilitation skills. After a few weeks, I sent a short email, curious to know what

> worked for her and where changes might be helpful. Shortly after when we spoke, she said, "Carolyn, you can be intense!" Initially, I was taken aback, and if I'm being honest, it was deflating. I had been going out of my way to stay connected because I wanted her to see the level of enthusiasm I had for our work together. I learned that my intensity was overbearing and didn't provide the regenerative space or processing time she preferred. Once I understood my impact, I could mindfully show up in our working relationship without my needs dominating our interactions.

I appreciate that self-awareness doesn't always come with the ease that this example appears to have. It takes time to learn how to ask for feedback in a way that is understood by the other person to be genuine and not just ask for the equivalent of an "everything's fine" response. Similarly, when you do get heavy, difficult feedback, understanding how to process it and learn from it without crushing your spirit or enthusiasm for the work will take some time.

Part of increasing our self-awareness comes with an understanding that this isn't about adding judgment or blame about our past or current behaviors; we need to acknowledge where we haven't been at our best and use our new tools of awareness to improve how we move forward.

This isn't a quest for perfection either; it's quite the opposite. It's an acknowledgment that we will continue to grow and evolve. If these concerns are coming up for you, that's okay. We need to be kind to ourselves in these moments of growth. If it's creating some resistance, know that it's likely a protective mechanism.

SELF-REGULATION: STAYING IN CONTROL

We expect leaders to be rational and objective as they lead teams through these turbulent times. The problem is that we are irrational human beings—we can't sidestep our emotions by turning off our limbic system. What we can do is accept emotions as data points and learn how to work with them.

I talked earlier in this book about what happens when your nervous system is activated in times of stress or trauma responses. Self-regulation is increasing the ability to keep your nervous system calm. In *The Quaking of America: An Embodied Guide to Navigating Our Nation's Upheaval and Racial Reckoning*, author Resmaa Menakem notes, "[a] calm, settled body is the foundation for health, for healing, for helping others, and for changing the world."[5]

Being calm means you're not being overtaken by your limbic system and not in "fight or flight" mode. You're able to understand and acknowledge your emotions to keep your reactivity low. This means you are curious, open, and not defensive with your response. It means you aren't activating stress responses in your colleagues or team members either—you aren't dumping your emotions on someone else. Self-regulation also means stopping your brain's natural instinct to fill in any gaps in the story that it believes might exist. You must check for facts. Let's look at an example.

Picture it: You're walking down the hall at work, and your boss, Freddie, walks past you without saying hello.

Without a self-regulation practice, before you can stop to consider the situation, your brain is already telling you that Freddie must be angry with you—they always greet people. Because information is missing, your brain fills in the gaps and you start thinking about all the various interactions you've had with Freddie over the past few weeks, wondering what might have caused them to ignore you. Immediately, you start to feel your heart rate increase (stress response), and you spend the rest of the day in a state of heightened anxiety.

With a self-regulation practice, as soon as you feel your heart rate increasing and your brain questioning what might have happened, you use a breathing technique to bring you back into the present moment. You remind yourself that you've worked with Freddie for a long time, and you're leaping to conclusions unnecessarily. Self-regulation will help you catch yourself in the moment to look at the situation logically and realize that there may be a number of reasons why they didn't say hello, but none of them relate to their thoughts or opinions about you.

So many of our unproductive relationships at work are based on overreactions and lack of self-regulation. Our brains add details to a situation and create a story—many times it's not built on facts and instead from our unconscious emotional patterns.

Here are some practices to help you strengthen your ability to self-regulate:

Expand your emotions vocabulary

Learning an expanded set of words to describe what you're feeling can help you better process what is happening and reduce its intensity, giving you more access to clear thoughts. Most people can only describe what they are feeling in the moment with one of these words: *mad, glad, sad*. I use this feelings wheel from Geoffrey Roberts to expand vocabulary and practice labeling emotions in the moment. The goal is to label the feeling, not judge it. You're not seeking a correct answer with this exercise, it's simply a way to consider new words to describe how you're feeling, and this image helps you make those connections.

Let's use the situation with Freddie as an example.

Start with the middle circle and pick one of the seven words. Let's say you felt **angry**.

Now look at the section in the concentric ring connected to **angry**. Do any of these words better describe how you're feeling?

Let's say that **frustrated** was a better description.

Then take one more look at the last concentric ring connected to **frustrated**.

Now you can consider **annoyed** or **infuriated**.

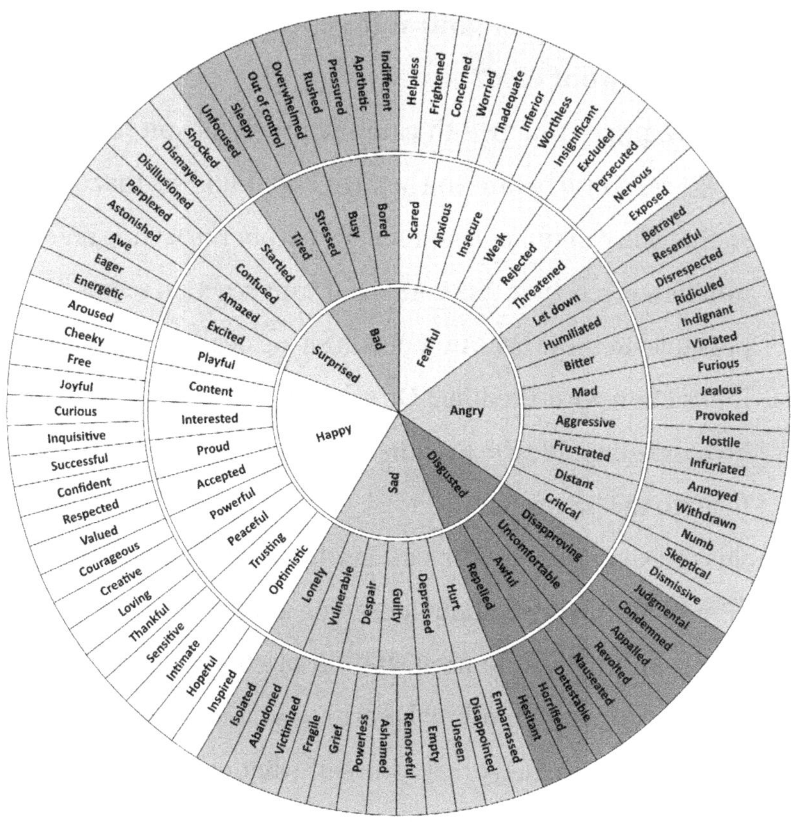

Source: Geoffrey Roberts, https://imgur.com/q6hcgsH. Found at https://feelingswheel.com/

According to Marc Brackett, author of *Permission to Feel: Unlocking the Power of Emotions to Help Our Kids, Ourselves, and Our Society Thrive*, "[w]e need the ability to experience and express all emotions, to down- or up-regulate both pleasant and unpleasant emotions in order to achieve greater well-being, make the most informed decisions, build and maintain meaningful relationships, and realize our potential."[6]

Pause as you feel yourself reacting in a situation and ask, what else?

This requires practice to catch yourself as you feel your stress response before you act. It's about finding that space so that you can unhook and separate from the feeling before mindlessly reacting. Ask yourself if your reaction seems proportional to the event. Am I making a big deal about a chance interaction with Freddie? Or ask yourself what else might be happening. Maybe Freddie was tired, or focused, or had to go to the bathroom.

Susan David refers to this as emotional agility. She writes, "Emotional agility is about loosening up, calming down, and living with more intention. It's about choosing how you'll respond to your emotional warning system."[7] As you find yourself feeling angry, ask yourself what else could you be feeling to see if expanded definitions help you pinpoint what's upsetting you.

Self-regulation is about helping your body understand when a stress response is happening and helping reconnect back to feelings of safety and security.

CO-REGULATION: MANAGING OUR CONNECTION WITH OTHERS

When we're self-aware and able to self-regulate, our last step is to be more aware of how our behavior is impacting others, and specifically, if it has the potential to create a stress response in other people.

It's important to note though that this doesn't mean you are responsible for the responses of others or need to be assessing or diagnosing if a traumatic event has occurred in someone's past. Your responsibility is to consider how your behavior might affect others you are working with directly and act in ways that keep stress triggers from happening in your interactions. As the CTRI notes, "we co-create safe environments when everyone in the organization takes on a responsibility to make safe decisions, and people believe others have their best interests in mind."[8]

This is where it's essential for you as a leader to recognize that people need safety and consistency to model vulnerability. Your self-awareness and self-regulation skills will be paramount to creating the psychological safety for your team to feel comfortable with taking risks and being more open.

In today's workplace, no one works in isolation. We have to collaborate, share ideas, and explore perspectives. Ideas need to be vetted with managers, and we have feedback loops in place to ensure stakeholder needs are being met. There's a lot of interaction between people in our workplaces.

How do people behave in meetings when you're leading them? This is a great way to understand your co-regulation skills. Is everyone quiet? Are people yelling at each other? It's very much influenced by you, whether you realize it or not.

This is where our body center of intelligence is hard at work. It's gathering input from your five senses and tuning in to the actions of others, looking for favorable responses, or determining threats and risks. As author Deb Dana notes, "[t]his social engagement system is both a sending system and a receiving system, constantly uploading and downloading information about connection. You are continuously posting information about yourself and gathering information about others."[9] Your behavior always impacts others through cues and signals. People either feel safe and coregulate with you, or they will turn to protective reactions or the guarded behaviors from Chapter 7.

When we don't accept the body and nervous system as a center of intelligence, we can too easily overlook the magnitude of our impact on other people. There's a disconnect for many leaders here. Relationships truly are the glue that hold our workplaces together and are often sacrificed so we can meet corporate objectives at all costs. When we lose sight of building connection with each other, it impacts our ability to feel safe. In *The Deepest Well*, author Nadine Burke Harris notes that the more you focus on healing steps like building healthy relationships, the more you will reduce stress hormones and increase your neuroplasticity.[10]

Our companies aren't built to settle our nervous systems. They are built to innovate, serve others, and generate profits. We have some really big societal problems to solve, so how do we temper the need for innovation and creativity without burning out and exploiting our people? Right now, it feels like we are designing our organizations to maximize the agitation in our systems. If we don't acknowledge where hierarchical power structures are limiting our performance, then it will appear that co-regulation isn't necessary.

In Chapter 7, I talked about the performance review process, but it bears repeating. Managers usually bring arbitrary notes and examples to this once- or twice-a-year process designed to highlight strengths and areas for improvement. This feedback is often based on the past few weeks of work, which ends up invalidating the experience for the recipient.

Imagine instead if the performance review was in service to the employee and worked to reduce a sense of conflict or triggering stress responses in order to increase the individual's ability to participate effectively in the discussion. This can happen; I've seen it in organizations where performance is openly discussed in ongoing conversations between manager and employee. Both parties have equal power, they share perspectives from various sources, and they prioritize this time to ensure a performance gap doesn't happen. This way corrections can be made faster and with more acceptance.

Regular behaviors, when intentionally demonstrated, can help create calmer conditions. Here are actions that signal safety to each center of intelligence.[11] They are especially useful when your dominant center is taking over. You can seek them yourself and proactively lead with them.

> **The head center feels safe when**: knowing the bigger picture before the details, understanding rationale without being interrupted by emotion, connecting the dots, practicing complex thinking, using paradoxical practices
>
> **The body center feels safe when**: seeing someone walking the talk, taking action without too much talking, discussing what is right and wrong, witnessing the existence

of order and clarity, recognizing that transparency is present and congruence takes place

The heart center feels safe when: discussing impact on individuals, expressing in general, showing their passion, being positive, feeling connection to others, mirroring back what they hear and see

Other co-regulation practices include:

Checking in/out at the start/end of meetings

Asking each person to share a word that describes how they're feeling at the start of a meeting and again at the end of the meeting can help establish group norms for behavior as well as determine if your own behaviors are negatively impacting others. I know I highlighted this in the previous chapter, but it's worth repeating. It's a simple action that shifts us out of "icebreaker" mentality and into a connective state that can signal safety to the nervous system.

Listening and validating more than correcting

In one-on-ones with your team, or in team meetings, focus more on what others are saying and find ways to echo or support their contributions rather than telling them what to do differently. Acknowledgment and validation go a long way in creating safety. This isn't about avoiding conflict or allowing poor performance to continue unchecked. Most of the time, we're asking for changes from team members because their approach isn't how we would do a task, rather than seeking out a valid reason why other approaches won't work.

Give space between back-to-back meetings
It's tempting to want to jump into the agenda, even when you know people have rushed from other meetings to get to their next one with you. However, giving everyone a few minutes upfront to grab a drink or simply sit to catch their breath helps them return to a calmer state. At Grantbook, a tech company that helps not-for-profits manage their philanthropy systems, meetings run from :10 minutes after the hour for only 50 minutes to give everyone 10 minutes of transition time in between meetings.

There is something very important and foundational to these Evolved Leader principles. It's the ability to be present and in the moment, also referred to as mindfulness. This is not a skill that is easily honed in today's fast-paced environment. All too often I hear, "I don't have time" or "I can't sit still that long" or "it doesn't work for me." If this is you, chances are you identified with several of the archetypes in Chapter 7.

Mindfulness practices send calming signals to your nervous system, which in turn help reduce blood pressure, heart rate, and cortisol levels in the body. Try to spend a few minutes (even if it's only one) at the start, middle, and end of your workday to quiet your mind and see what thoughts surface. If your body is calm, your mind will follow.

In the next chapter, I'll share daily practices to help you find more presence and stillness. I promise it's not about slowing life to a snail's pace. I know you've got a lot of responsibilities to juggle. These are practical things that you can do every day, without needing to sit still.

REFLECTIONS ON YOUR EVOLVED LEADERSHIP JOURNEY

1. What's your typical response when receiving feedback? Can you accept positive feedback and constructive criticism? Are you open, defensive, or dismissive? Does it change depending on who is giving it to you?

2. Use a tool to track your emotions for one week by picking random moments in the day. Consider mapping them to a feelings wheel or in an app. Did you see any interesting patterns? Did you notice any thought patterns associated with certain emotions?

3. What is one co-regulation practice listed in this chapter that you are willing to try and do more often? What differences did you notice in yourself and the team?

CHAPTER 10

DAILY PRACTICES FOR EVOLVED LEADERS

You've likely heard the oxygen mask metaphor in resilience workshops and conversations about burnout. It picks up on the safety announcements that we hear at the start of every flight, reminding us that in an emergency, we need to take time to put on our own oxygen mask before helping other people. We use that metaphor as a beacon of self-care and as a reminder to support our own mental health so we don't reach a point where we won't be able to help anyone else, including ourselves.

I understand why people use the metaphor; it quickly and easily makes the point about prioritizing our own health, something many of us don't do. However, it misses one key detail. There's no point in putting on an oxygen mask if there isn't any oxygen flowing through it.

During my years as a corporate leader, I thought my oxygen mask was always on. I was a professional oxygen-mask wearer, doing an excellent job of showing everyone that I was coping. I was working excessively, putting pressure on myself to meet every deadline and overachieve. I thought I was a great leader because I had good relationships with everyone on my team and with colleagues in other functional areas and roles across the company. I was *crushing* the oxygen mask.

It's only recently that I've started to understand that while I was likely a good leader, I wasn't outstanding. I was over-relying on strong relationships while ignoring other aspects that strong leaders need. I wasn't great at tough performance conversations; I avoided them. I wasn't willing to be open and vulnerable with my team; they knew we just needed to push through whatever crisis was in front of us. I was inconsistent in taking care of my mental, physical, and emotional health. I was good enough on the outside, but I was a mess on the inside. I thought I was doing a great job, but it was only because I had a large capacity and could take on a lot.

We've learned as leaders why we need to put on our own oxygen mask first. The problem is, we don't always know if the oxygen is flowing. We need to learn how to keep this oxygen flow at a steady stream instead of breathing in stale air. The work to continue to cultivate self-awareness and increase your capacity for self-regulation and co-regulation needs to be a continual, daily priority. It's when you think you don't need the practice anymore that you need to double down on it.

I started to focus on building my own daily practice about nine years ago. A group of corporate directors read the book *Finding the Space to Lead* by Janice Marturano. Mindfulness was just starting to become an acceptable topic at work, and our director team read the book and discussed it at a lunch 'n learn. I enjoyed the experience and remember thinking it might be a valuable skill to build. I began experimenting with different mindfulness apps and found my way to Headspace. I started with just two minutes of quietly listening to the instructions and trying to tune out the noise in my head. I felt no pressure to sit for the thirty minutes or more that I kept hearing suggested from the experts; I committed to simply try for a few minutes each day. I would miss some days, but I would keep pulling myself back to the practice. Slowly, the practice took hold, and I was sitting in a present state for a few minutes each day.

Mindfulness apps can help you with increasing the time and consistency of your practice. I was able to increase my time by a few minutes each week until I was consistently practicing mindfulness meditation for fifteen minutes a day.

I started to notice small differences in my day when I committed to this practice in the morning. If I sat quietly for those assigned minutes, I could think a little more clearly throughout the day. I felt calmer and less distracted, and I was less easily frustrated. At one point I could achieve forty-five minutes of stillness, but I'll be honest: that's been a hard habit to maintain.

Being stuck in lockdown helped me carve out time to make this habit stick and become more consistent. I replaced my commuting with spending more time in silence using the app. It helped that my kids were older and didn't need my assistance in the mornings, but I felt the benefits so strongly and so soon after starting to make it a habit that I likely would have found pockets in my day to do this practice when the kids were younger.

At the same time, I started seeking silence while out walking. Previously, I had loved the idea of multitasking while walking the dog, and I would listen to audiobooks or podcasts or move some of my virtual calls from my computer to my phone. I decided to seek out more quiet time while out for walks, listening to the voice in my own head instead of what others wanted me to absorb.

WHY YOU NEED A DAILY PRACTICE

While stress responses activate your sympathetic nervous system, calming practices like meditation activate your parasympathetic nervous system, which some call "rest and digest."

I do my best now to do at least one or two practices every day. I make sure that each day starts intentionally with one of them, so my day begins at a calm pace rather than a "wildly hectic, roll out of bed and race to get everything done" pace.

It's an evolution that is done in steps rather than all at once. Doing so allows us to work in the full expression of ourselves and hopefully help others do the same. We imagine that thinking about calming our system might be enough, but it needs to be a physical practice. As author and psychotherapist Resmaa Menakem notes, "[b]ecause trauma is developed by the body, it needs to be healed and metabolized within the body. Cognitive practices alone, such as talk therapy, can be helpful, but they usually aren't sufficient."[1]

We need to regulate our nervous systems with intention. As we continue with these practices, we're able to rewire how our bodies respond during those same stressors that deregulated us. As author and medical doctor Nadine Burke Harris notes, the more we do these stress-reducing practices, "the more you'll reduce stress hormones, reduce inflammation, enhance neuroplasticity, and delay cellular aging."[2] For her patients, there are six things she recommends: sleep, exercise, nutrition, mindfulness, mental health, and healthy relationships.[3]

I'm not saying your daily practice will eliminate all the stress in your life, or even be able to remove all your stress responses. Meditating for hours a day still can't achieve that. But these practices will help you significantly in how you respond to those stressors in the moment and in the time that follows. You'll see a reduction in the intensity of those reactions, keeping you closer to your regulated state.

CONNECTING TO YOUR CENTERS OF INTELLIGENCE

Authors Sharon Ball and Renée Siegel recommend the "Three-M Triad"[4] to bring your nervous system back into regulation—the practices of movement, mindfulness, and meaningful connections that can keep you grounded and resilient. Each of these tactics connects to a specific center of intelligence: movement for focusing on the body center, meditation for the head center, and meaningful connections for the heart center. I learned from their work that developing an integrated practice can help bring awareness to gaps you might not otherwise see, particularly for those centers where you aren't dominant.

Ball and Siegel outline a series of excellent questions[5] for checking in with your center of intelligence to understand what you need in the current moment. Regardless of your dominant type, you can use any of these practices, which can bring balance and allow you to access the insight from each center.

To check in with your body center, ask yourself:

- How does movement address my need for power and control?
- What am I doing to keep my body moving now?
- Are there ways I can move and exercise that I might try?
- What do I have control over?
- What do I have control over that I am not controlling and need to?
- What is out of my control?
- What am I attempting to control that is not helpful or healthy for me?

To check in with your heart center, ask yourself:

- How do meaningful connections address my need for esteem and affirmation?

- Who am I spending time with?
- Are they supportive, nurturing, and accepting?
- Who could I be spending time with that I'm not?
- How can I connect with others that I'm not doing right now?
- How am I offering support to others important to me?

To check in with your head center, ask yourself:

- How does mindfulness address my need for safety, security, and certainty?
- What is safe in my life now?
- What is predictable in my life now?
- What am I certain about now?
- Am I spending too much time listening to the news?
- If I am in danger, do I have a plan?
- Who can I count on to help me if I have a problem?

Asking yourself these questions, or starting with questions like "As I scan my head, heart, and body centers, what gaps am I sensing? What do I need in this moment?" will help lead you to the right practice.

PRACTICES FOR EVERY DAY

Individually, each of these practices I describe next looks like a small thing that has helped bring me into the present moment. It's hard work to break from the cycle of busyness; I'm not going to sugarcoat it.

I started by leaving my phone out of my bedroom, which was

transformative just on its own. I do my best to leave it in the kitchen at 9 p.m. until the next morning. Any emergency important enough to disturb my sleep can come through on the landline. Having my phone out of sight and out of mind did wonders for settling my nervous system.

If this feels like too much, then here's a modified version. Put your phone on Do Not Disturb mode and place it in the room where you can't reach it while lying in bed. You can tag important contacts so their calls will come through. Just make sure your boss isn't on that list!

MEDITATION

Meditation is the process of calming the mind through a series of actions (like breathing) or guided instructions. Personally, I like to use the word *mindfulness*, as it helps me connect to the purpose of this practice—to be present in the moment. It's hard to be in the moment when you're consumed by thoughts of the past or worrying about the future. This keeps your mind overly active and unable to tolerate stillness. It's in the stillness where we can find deeper insights and trust our instincts to be true.

If sitting still seems like too much, then try being meditative in an activity like walking or doing the dishes. Focus on your senses as you do the activity. What do you smell? What do you feel?

BREATHWORK

Learning simple breathing techniques can be one of the fastest ways to calm your stress reactions without requiring props or changing your environment. You can google these to learn a wide range of ways to change your stress levels by breathing differently in the moment.

One of the simplest practices I teach to people in my workshops is box breathing:

- Breathe in for 4 seconds
- Hold for 4 seconds
- Breathe out for 4 seconds
- Hold for 4 seconds

Put this book down for a moment and try a few cycles. Notice how your breathing and heart rate change (if they don't, that's okay too!). Notice if your sense of urgency or anxiousness is altered at all.

The other practice I like to teach people for calming their nervous system is the 4-7-8 exercise:

- Breathe in for 4 seconds
- Hold for 7 seconds
- Breathe out for 8 seconds

This one is particularly helpful to bring you closer to a state of sleep, but it also works for calming down or preparing for a difficult meeting or conversation. Try it in different settings or situations and see what helps and when.

There are breathing practices you can do on the ground with your hand on your diaphragm or with your hands flat on your desk in front of you to ground you. You can even do mindful breathing at a stoplight or while sitting in traffic.

NATURE

For many people, walking in nature can have a calming effect on the nervous system. Be outside, disconnected from technology and screens. Some have started forest bathing or *shinrin-yoku*, a practice first developed in Japan to absorb the calming environment that walking in the woods can create. Don't worry, you aren't actually "bathing," and your clothes stay on.

This is one of my favorite practices and my walks became longer and longer during the height of the pandemic. Whether it's the wind in the leaves or seeing the interconnection of the tree roots to remind us of the communities we're part of, walking in nature can have different reactions in each of us. As Deb Dana notes, "[c]reativity often blossoms in solitude, as does the self-reflection that leads to self-transformation."[6]

ART AND MUSIC

I can tell you that I am not an artist, but I don't let that keep me from using art and music in my somatic practices from time to time.

The use of art tools like crayons, paints, or even yarn for knitting can have immediate calming effects. It's why knitting needles and yarn baskets are often found in hospital waiting rooms. And coloring books for adults have exploded since 2013 when Johanna Basford published *Secret Garden*, the first book that led to the trend.

For some people, it's the ability to stay disconnected from devices that makes art pursuits so appealing; for others, it's the repetitive motions that have a calming effect. This practice requires some space and perhaps is less conducive to the workplace, but it's still worth exploring.

Music carries a range of frequencies that can influence our moods. You might already notice a preference in music depending on your mood. Follow your instinct and consider trying out new genres. They might bring a different sense of calm to you. Have you tried classical, jazz, nature, cinematic, chill? Many streaming services have playlists with "best of" sets on any topic you can imagine. My favorite highlights "the most relaxing songs of all time" according to science.

Recently, I've been using an app to play different frequency sounds in my office and at home to create various moods. In fact, it's playing in my earbuds as I write this chapter. These become energies I can feel in my body, and they also activate parts of my brain. Also, listening to a sound bath that uses vibrations or sound bowls can create a sense of calm or lead to deeper, purposeful breathing.

WRITING

For years, I avoided journal writing because I thought I was doing it wrong. I found it hard to know what to write about, or if I did manage to sit down and write a few lines, the words felt awkward when I read them back.

It was spending time with my friend Stephanie Woodward that helped me develop a deeper journaling practice. She started by sharing some questions to ask myself each time I sat down to write, including:

- What did I learn today?
- What surprised me today?
- What disappointed me today?
- What am I grateful for today?

These simple questions helped me unlock a journal practice that I've been able to continue several times a week for a few years.

Journaling is an important part of your self-regulation practice to track emotions and explore what they might be telling you. I've used the How We Feel app that allows me to track and color-code my emotions, so I can look for patterns and any common triggers to try and avoid in the future. I've also used the Permission to Feel app from Oji Life Lab.

MOVEMENT

I do body scans daily to understand what sensations I'm feeling and what feels like it's missing. It took a long time for me to get to this point.

Lots of physical activities are still available online, even as gyms and fitness centers opened back up after the pandemic lockdown. Programming like personal training or Pilates, which felt difficult to offer remotely prior to COVID, has moved to virtual and asynchronous modes.

I try to walk every day, even if it's only a short walk around the block with my dog. I also see my trainer for strength training once a week. The sky's the limit; do whatever works for your personal and physical situation.

There's a wide range of ways to build a daily practice that feeds your somatic needs—entire books have been dedicated to the subject. Play with different forms, times of day, and combinations. Take your journal into the woods or down by the lake. Find a friend and start a regular walking routine. Experiment with paints or Tibetan singing bowls.

Do what feels right and stick with it. Or make a commitment to a time of day and mix it up. Remember, the point isn't to push yourself to such a level of calm that you're feeling numb or hope to be entirely non-reactive. As Lesser notes, "[f]eel all of your feelings. Feel anger, love, fear, grief, courage, wonder, joy. Feel all of it because somewhere in that soup is your wisdom and your guidance. Letting yourself feel is different from acting on those feelings."[7]

These practices will help you improve the principles of self-regulation and co-regulation, particularly when you regularly include meditation. Don't be afraid to explore them, even if unexpected emotions pop up at times. As Menakem says, "[h]ealing and growth always involve discomfort. But so does refusing to heal or grow."[8]

REFLECTIONS ON YOUR EVOLVED LEADERSHIP JOURNEY

1. What resistance comes up for you about daily practices? What do you feel, think and sense in your body when reflecting on this topic?

2. I shared questions to check in with the different centers of intelligence in this chapter. Choose one center and ask yourself the questions a few times during the week. What insight do they provide?

3. Pick one practice that's new for you and try it once a day for a week. What impact did it have?

CHAPTER 11

AN INVITATION TO EVOLVE

In the months since I created the Evolved Leader framework, and in writing this book, I've been talking about the concepts and sharing the model with clients and people I've met in my travels, including people attending my workshops, speaking engagements, or even those at the airport. I was excited to share the concepts before this book was written and published and to hear their reactions and questions back to me.

Almost every person has said a version of the following: "This makes so much sense. I need to focus on myself first, then see how that can improve my leadership and the dynamics within my team." Each of them has seen and acknowledged that the demands for them as leaders have changed significantly since the start of the pandemic, and likely will for some time.

The changes I describe in this book—understanding centers of intelligence, the impact of trauma, and learning the principles and practices to create a calm, connected leadership style—won't happen overnight. It will take a conscious effort to evolve, and it can't happen all at once.

I've been building a somatic practice and deepening my self-awareness for several years now, well before I'd even conceived of the Evolved Leader concept. Once I understood how my body was an unrecognized center of intelligence, I became committed to reconnecting with it, including adding activities to help calm my nervous system. Slowly but surely, things started to fall into place. I found I wasn't immediately reactive to negative feedback or arguments from my kids or my husband. I was open to hearing feedback from clients about my programs without immediately overreacting; I could ask them for suggestions for ways to improve future sessions, and they were able to provide them without worrying that I was going to be upset.

The biggest change to resisting the busyness of life has come from my daily practices. It continues to evolve as I test new activities. I subscribe to different apps that provide varying types of meditation, from spoken words with designed outcomes to a mix of sounds that immediately transport me to the ocean.

Certain practices only last for a while, and I find myself looking for new options from time to time. I don't take it as a signal that it is no longer working for me; I use it as an opportunity to look inward and consider what else my head, heart, and body are needing at that moment. There are times when I feel drawn to be more still, and other times I get that signal that I need to do more physically to help balance my cognitive and emotional burdens.

I've also worked with coaches and psychotherapists who specialize in somatic therapies. This has been a conscious choice to do deeper work with my body and restore the mind–body connection back to a healthier state.

I'm determined to continue sustaining my Evolved Leader work because of the changes I'm seeing outside of work as well. It's not perfect, but perfection isn't the goal. The practices need to happen daily because we continue to falter or fall back on old patterns. And just as we continue to evolve, so do the people around us. Our triggers might fade, and new ones might arise. As long as we do the work each day to stay grounded and keep our nervous systems regulated (to the best that we can), we'll continue to be able to navigate the changes that life brings us. And if we can help bring others along with us on our journey, we'll be able to help each other stay connected and calm as well.

It's a big ask, no question, but I hope you are already starting to see changes as you test out new practices.

TWO WAYS TO BEGIN: SMALL STEPS OR BIG BANG

For most people, there are two different instincts when looking at making changes in how we live our lives. We can commit to making a big change all at once, often on a significant date like January 1, where "from this day forward" we promise to ourselves to make a change, small or large. We anchor our intent to a significant date that gives us a sense of a fresh start.

But overnight changes are hard. We need to break through old thinking and triggers to uphold our commitment, which is why so many people see their New Year's resolutions fade before the end of January arrives—there's just too much friction in our daily lives to make bold changes stick.

Smaller changes are much more realistic, but they require stamina to maintain for a longer time frame. You might still be working on these changes six months or a year later.

What do small changes look like for an Evolved Leader? Finding tiny ways to commit to a daily practice. It could be five minutes of slow breathing or meditation when you first wake up or right after you brush your teeth. Attaching your practice to something you're already doing means the reminder to practice will automatically happen. When I let the dog outside, I know my meditation time will follow.

When it comes to creating new habits, we can get wrapped up in goal setting and trying to be the best. In your journey of Evolved Leadership, how you achieve those goals is just as important. That's the secret to making changes stick: creating a system of routines, rituals, and practices. In his book *Atomic Habits*, James Clear states "Ultimately, it is your commitment to the process that will determine your progress."[1]

What you're *actually* committing to is to continuing to practice and evolve your mastery skills on a daily basis. That's what you're changing—you're no longer imagining that your self-improvement work will be finished.

PUSHING THROUGH RESISTANCE: THE HERO(INE)'S JOURNEY

I don't know anything about where you work or the type of team you lead, but I can say with one-hundred-percent certainty that adjusting to change is part of your reality. No one I've encountered in recent years has any degree of certainty or lack of looming change. Even if the business is in a steady environment or industry, there are outside and inside forces that threaten the status quo every day. And of course, COVID has meant change has increased too. It can be a roller coaster, and it's a journey.

Working in an ever-changing environment can, ironically, create significant amounts of resistance to change. Rather than getting comfortable with it, we resent it and try to keep it out of our lives. It's partly because we are just so tired. The resistance is also based on the reality that we crave stability and consistency. I believe that people don't really resist change, they just need a bit of time to grieve what they are losing, and we don't often give ourselves this time.

The Hero's Journey,[2] first written as the "Monomyth" by Joseph Campbell in 1949, outlined universal steps in the process of change we all experience. In the first phase, there's the moment where the hero (for our purposes, this person can be any gender) chooses to set out on this path of discovery—they feel a calling, or sense that a concern or challenge in their life could be solved.

Perhaps that's where you are today. You're ready to implement the ideas and practices you learned from this book. You might feel some resistance internally as you start to practice, and that's okay. You are ready to explore what it could be like to lead from a different place, and you make the commitment to yourself to do the work needed to lead differently.

In the second phase of the Hero's Journey, this commitment to change is challenged. Perhaps you have trouble sticking to your new daily practices, or you find yourself unable to self- or co-regulate during difficult situations at work. As you start to test the practices and are mindful of keeping your nervous system regulated throughout the day, you're stepping into a new phase of learning. You might seek out mentors who can help you stick to the commitment you've made, even if it's an unpopular choice. You might find that others don't agree with your choices, or they might encourage you to stick with your old habits. Staying the course can be difficult, but as you work through the resistance and challenges, the rewards become clearer.

In the last phase of this learning quest of the Hero's Journey, you return to your day-to-day life, rewards in hand, and share what you've learned with others during your learning journey.

The challenge with this model is that it keeps the hero isolated from everyone else. Throughout the journey, it's described in the language of individual choices and reliance only on the self in order to complete the quest.

To expand this viewpoint, there are lessons we can learn from the Heroine's Journey,[3] which was created in 1983 by Maureen Murdock, a student of Campbell's. Murdock understood that a woman's experience through a similar path had different lessons to offer. It follows a similar arc of stepping into the journey, but it involves finding allies much earlier in the process and an understanding that the systems we work within can provide us with allies as well as blocks. It's an important aspect to integrate into our work journeys, regardless of gender.

The Heroine's Journey also shows us that in some cases, the "reward" can be experienced earlier, but there is still work to be done well after that point. We might see the benefits of our Evolved Leadership skills with our team, but we still have work to do—to share what we've learned with other leaders in the organization.

Having an awareness of how these systems can encourage and impede our choice to change how we lead can help us as we practice our new skills as evolved leaders.

I should mention here that the Heroine's Journey has a feminist lens, which can provide some insights as warranted, but that's not my purpose for mentioning it. I'm interested in learning from all experiences in change so as to help make the path forward easier for each of us.

These journeys are storytelling devices and a reminder of the shared experiences of many others who have worked through difficult times. They can help us remember that this process of learning and change, once we choose to begin, can be challenging. We can encounter resistance and attempts from others to throw us off course. But when we persevere, the rewards can be significant.

Every journey starts with a first step. What will yours be?

CREATING A MOVEMENT OF EVOLVED LEADERS

I've seen how this practice can change people and create a new level of ease in their lives. Leaders who spend every day in challenging discussions with their teams and their own managers are able to be authentic by reducing their reactivity and choosing curiosity to stay open and present.

My hope is for a groundswell of evolved leaders to forge a path for what leadership needs to be as we meet the new expectations set by employees today who have different parameters for what work needs to look like than they did before COVID. It's the intensity of the pandemic and everything that was taken from us during lockdowns and isolation at home that is leaving people feeling fragile. Brittle. Not able to handle even "one more little thing."

It's our job as leaders to show up as calm, grounded, and energized. We can't expect others to do it first. Our own trauma will keep disrupting us from building strong, productive relationships with our teams if we don't commit to evolve.

As we step into this work together, I hope we can have new conversations about what leadership needs to be now and support each other in committing to doing the daily practices that keep us evolving.

I look forward to your stories; I hope you'll share your wins and your struggles on this new path. I hope you'll help each other stay connected to your centers of intelligence. I hope you'll find new somatic practices that help you stay grounded.

Let's become human spirit ignitors and evolve leadership together.

REFLECTIONS ON YOUR EVOLVED LEADERSHIP JOURNEY

1. Think of a behavior change or new habit you were successful with in the past. What system of routines, rituals, or cues were in place? How can you apply learnings from that experience to your own Evolved Leadership journey?

2. What resistance comes up for you with Evolved Leadership? What might help you work through it?

3. What excites you about Evolved Leadership? How will you capitalize on it?

AFTERWORD

"If we are peaceful, if we are happy, we can smile and blossom like a flower, and everyone in our family, our entire society, will benefit from our peace."

–Thich Nhat Hanh[1]

The water from the Atlantic Ocean gently whispers up the shore to meet my feet. Every tender passing wave takes a little of the sand away with it. The sand goes quietly, without putting up a fight, like an agreement between the water and the land that I'm not privy to: if you must go, take me with you.

The subtle shushing of the ocean in my ears rocks me to my core. I know this sound. I know this beach. As my feet slowly sink into the disappearing ground beneath me, the tears start to fall.

Softly at first. But as soon as I accept them, they begin to pour, of course.

They are a symphony of conflicting emotions. A concoction of sadness, of anger, of happiness, of chaos, of peace. All at once. And also, surprisingly, gratitude. I can't believe I'm here, and I'm in awe of the journey I've endured.

I'm in Punta Cana, on one of the most pristine beaches in the Dominican Republic, with the man I love. The sun is slowly advancing above the horizon, making its claim once again.

Twenty years ago—almost to the day—I was on this same island in the Caribbean on a honeymoon. I was filled with so much promise about the future. Little did I know about the massive storm that lie ahead.

Loosening my grip on the reins of life and surrendering to the flow of what is in the moment has been the hardest thing I've ever done. I stopped running, and I faced fear and grief. The busyness was too exhausting.

The breeze blows my long hair, and I reach up to pull it behind my ears so I can stay fixated on the skyline. The colors are almost impossible to witness. Pinks and oranges and purples and, right above me, dark blue, where the sky resists the turning of night to day.

The light gets brighter as the sun ascends into the sky and a warm, comfortable sense of peace runs through me. I know deeply that while storms will never disappear from my life, I'm now able to weather them with new power.

That moment on the beach changed the direction of this book and the energy with which I created it. But my intention behind the words has never changed. Every time I sat down to write, speak, and edit any piece of this work, I had my sons in mind.

So, in honor of doing things upside down, here I am finishing this book as I had always intended to start it. With a letter to you both. My boys.

Andrew & Ayden,

I've thought of you two throughout this entire process.

I'd visualize your little baby noses and those bright, innocent eyes staring up at me, grateful and safe in my arms while slurping up a bottle. I can still smell the fresh newborn hair and conjure up that same feeling of your soft cheek against my cheek. I'd feel the boundless energy bouncing through your toddler years, the chasing and the learning and the stumbling and the giggles and the laughter. Much of your childhood was a blur, but I'm eternally grateful for what I can remember. I was becoming so much of myself then, when you two were becoming your own selves, too.

It's hard to deal with grief when you have two little people to care for and raise. Actually, it's impossible. I didn't really deal with it. I simply coped. I did it the best way I knew how, but I was consumed with comparison and judgment. My one mission then was to give you a "normal" childhood. I realize now that nobody has really figured out what that even means.

This writing process has brought me to a more profound understanding that my determination to over function throughout life has happened as a way to repress my grief. Your childhood didn't go as planned, and I did the best I could to adapt. And, wow, is parenthood the ultimate teacher.

Your actions get reflected back to you in real time. There is nowhere to hide. There's always something or someone or some new challenge pointing out the gaps, if you can see them. For many years of your life, I was unable to see the dissonance between my intentions and my impact. I'm grateful that I was able to close this gap before you left the house and started the next chapter of your life, on your own.

I think I speak for most parents when I say I want you to make the world a better place—to learn from the mistakes of previous generations, but to absorb their wisdom as well. To make your own glorious, beautiful, messy and perfect mistakes and to know that no matter what, it's okay. That you are human. You are brave. You are allowed to be imperfect.

You don't need to prove anything to anyone. And, in doing so, show others that it's safe to be imperfect, too.

With this next step into the world, I hope you can find your own authentic footprint. I hope you feel brave enough to walk it, to be kind, to be vulnerable, to be honest. I hope you have the compassion to meet others where they're at and remember that we're all just trying to do our best. And I hope you have the audacity to do it all your own way. Whatever that may be.

I trust along the way that you will bring much needed change to our workplaces. I trust that wherever you go and whomever you are surrounded by that you will be the ones who pioneer the radical gentleness that it takes to really be authentic.

You have already made me so proud. The evolution of our family, of you as men, and of our relationship has been the greatest gift of my life.

Thank you for being patient with me.
And thank you for being you.
Love you.
xoxox

ACKNOWLEDGMENTS

Several interesting characters have come in and out of my life throughout the past fifty years, shaping me to be the woman I am today. I'm grateful for what they've taught me and the lessons I've learned.

I'd like to acknowledge a special group who were instrumental in supporting me through the development of this book and the Evolve Leadership Model. Writing this book has been what I call a "therapeutic roller coaster," with exhilarating highs and exasperating lows. I wouldn't have made it through without their guidance, support, and love.

To my husband, Don, who has taught me that I can be loved with all my imperfections. You taught me how to slow down, you constantly challenge me, and you make me laugh unlike any other. Your love and support may be quiet and intellectual, but I feel it strongly and it doesn't go unnoticed. None of this would have been possible without you.

There's nothing that compares to a mother's love. Wally has been my pillar of strength and biggest cheerleader throughout my five decades of life. She has shown up at exactly the right time and stayed away when I needed to figure things out on my own. I'm truly blessed.

One thing my mom told me as a child was how special it is to find true friendship that lasts a lifetime. Big love to Nicole MacNeil, the calm, steady voice who has always believed in me (even in my biggest mess-ups) and saw what I could be, especially when I couldn't see it myself. And ginormous hugs to Jodi Murray. I didn't know I needed a protector, but thankfully back in grade 6, you knew I did. Thank you for being there throughout the years and giving me a soft place to land, literally and figuratively. You and Will have never stopped believing in me, and I'm incredibly grateful to you both for the countless late-night conversations. And to my Yoda, your wisdom and guidance over the years has given me great strength for which I'm forever grateful.

To Beatrice Chestnut and Uranio Paes, the best Enneagram teachers in the world. My personal journey in your retreats has been, in short, transformative. I felt your guidance and care every step of the way. From a professional perspective, you've taught me how to honor the Enneagram system and serve clients most ethically with it. I'm grateful to be part of your CP Enneagram Academy community and to be connected with other students and practitioners. Consider me a lifetime member.

Before I left the corporate world, I took community for granted. Thankfully, I fell into the world of Coralus (formerly SheEO) and was inspired by countless role models as I built my business. There isn't one person to single out; rather, it's a vast network that has shaped how I run my business and invest my time. I'm a socially minded entrepreneur because of their influence.

I also want to extend my deep gratitude to the BBEARG (Brené Brown Education and Research Group) community. I've learned how to hold space and inspire growth in meaningful ways through the Dare the Lead™ curriculum with the support of amazing practitioners around the world. It's a privilege to be part of this group and grow with you all.

On the publishing side, a huge thank you to Sabrina, Christine, and Doris at YGTMedia. I'm so grateful for your patience and support as I faced unexpected delays, pushed back deadlines, and evolved a rambling first manuscript into this beautiful book baby. Being part of your author community led to life-changing connections that have been instrumental in my personal and professional growth.

Leisse Wilcox is one of those beautiful and unexpected connections that catapulted my personal growth journey into a new dimension. The universe places people in your path for a reason. I'm incredibly grateful for your coaching and your kind-hearted challenge to expand my book beyond *The Perfect Widow*. Thank you for planting the seed and watering it.

To the creative souls who helped me shape ideas with their energy and talent: Lois McKenzie, you are the diamond who showed up precisely when I needed you. Thank you for all you've done on this journey with me and for what's to come. To John Nethersole, whose visual creative talent, brand direction, and wholehearted support has been invaluable with *Evolve* and since I started my business. And to Paris Grimmond and Jennifer Gardner for your dedication and commitment to get *Evolve* into the hands of leaders globally. I'm so thankful for everything you've done.

I could easily visualize all the components of this book in my head but making them coherent and flow together has been incredibly challenging. I'm so grateful to these people for the time they took to provide feedback on my manuscript: Valerie Atkins, Janet Watts, Tejal Neringer, Leanne Clarke, Krista Kay, and Lisa Burchartz. Your fingerprints are throughout these pages because I value your insight and experience. Integrating your suggestions took this book to a whole new level.

I wasn't sure if I would have a foreword in this book. Was the topic too edgy? Was there someone in my network who would have a good grasp of what I was trying to say? A huge thank you to Glain Roberts-McCabe who graciously accepted my request without hesitation. Thank you for not only writing such a beautiful foreword but also for the infrequent yet deep coffee discussions we've had over the past five years.

And finally, to Alyssa Burkus, the very talented architect and Lego builder who was an integral partner in bringing this book to life. Thank you from the bottom of my heart for your guidance and friendship.

RESOURCES

WORK WITH ME

If you've made it this far into the book, you are likely a dedicated and committed leader. I'd love to hear from you and perhaps explore an opportunity to work with you and your organization as a coach, facilitator, and/or speaker.

Website: https://www.carolynswora.com/
Instagram: @carolynswora
LinkedIn: Carolyn Swora
Email: support@carolynswora.com

BOOKS

Energetic Boundaries by Cyndi Dale

How We Work by Leah Weiss

The Language of Emotions: What Your Feelings Are Trying to Tell You by Karla McLaren

Stronger Through Adversity: World-Class Leaders Share Pandemic-Tested Lessons on Thriving During the Toughest Challenges by Joseph Michelli

Accessing the Healing Power of the Vagus Nerve by Stanley Rosenberg https://www.chapters.indigo.ca/en-ca/books/accessing-the-healing-power-of/9781623170240-item.html

The Complex PTSD Workbook: A Mind-Body Approach to Regaining Emotional Control and Becoming Whole by Arielle Schwartz, PhD

How to Do the Work by Dr. Nicole LePera

Friends with Your Mind: How to Stop Torturing Yourself with Your Thoughts (Breathe, Relax, Heal Book 1) by Lynn Fraser

Widen the Window by Elizabeth Stanley, PhD

Shine: Ignite Your Inner Game to Lead Consciously at Work and in the World by Carley Hauck
https://www.soundstrue.com/products/shine

AUDIO, VIDEOS, AND ONLINE COURSES

QiGong with David Beaudry of Noble Movement:
https://www.youtube.com/channel/UCfKhTracstwCOPcfhs3yEMg

Anchored - How to Befriend Your Nervous System Using Polyvagal Theory: Deb Dana
https://www.soundstrue.com/products/Anchored

Heal Your Nervous System by Dr. Linnea
https://healyournervoussystem.com/

Jess McQuire: Repairing the Nervous System: Vagus Nerve Training Chronic & Traumatic Stress Recovery. https://www.jessicamaguire.com

Awaken with Ally Wise: Life Transformation Mentor with a Focus on Self-Reconnection, Trauma Resolution and Nervous System Empowerment Mentorship Program and Workbook The Career Therapist: Lee McKay Doe, MBACP (specializes in the Fawn Trauma Response). Psychotherapist /Career Psychotherapy www.thecareertherapist.com

Dr. Jennifer Douglas. https://www.drjenniferdouglas.com/courses

Dr. Dan Siegel's Hand Model of the Brain (8 minutes) https://www.youtube.com/watch?v=f-m2YcdMdFw

Lynn Fraser (Somatic Mindfulness and trauma expert) has several free online offerings for healing complex trauma https://lynnfraserstillpoint.com/workshops/online-learning/

END NOTES

INTRODUCTION

1. "Burn-out an 'occupational phenomenon': International Classification of Diseases." World Health Organization, May 28, 2019. https://www.who.int/news/item/28-05-2019-burn-out-an-occupational-phenomenon-international-classification-of-diseases

CHAPTER 1

1. E. Beth Hemhill. "Uncomfortable (but Necessary) Conversations About Burnout." Gallup, December 6, 2022. https://www.gallup.com/workplace/406232/uncomfortable-necessary-conversations-burnout.aspx

2. Kerri Kelly, *American Detox: The Myth of Wellness and How We Can Truly Heal* (North Atlantic Books, 2022).
3. *State of Human Connection at Work: Findings from the Workhuman IQ Spring 2022 International Survey Report*. Workhuman. https://www.workhuman.com/resources/reports-guides/two-years-into-covid-the-state-of-human-connection-at-work.
4. David Rock. "We Need Time to Rehabilitate from the Trauma of the Pandemic." *Harvard Business Review*, February 7, 2022. https://hbr.org/2022/02/we-need-time-to-rehabilitate-from-the-trauma-of-the-pandemic
5. Tara Haelle. "Your 'Surge Capacity' Is Depleted, That's Why You Feel Awful." Elemental-Medium, August 17, 2020. https://elemental.medium.com/your-surge-capacity-is-depleted-it-s-why-you-feel-awful-de285d542f4c
6. Brené Brown, *Dare to Lead: Brave Work. Tough Conversations. Whole Hearts.* (Random House, 2018).
7. Kelly, *American Detox.*
8. Deloitte | LifeWorks. "Inspiring Insights: Well-being and resilience in senior leaders report." Deloitte. 2021.
9. Mental Health Commission of Canada. *National Standard for Psychological Health & Safety in the Workplace (the Standard)*. 2013. https://mentalhealthcommission.ca/national-standard/
10. ACES Facts. TraumaInstituteinternational.com https://traumainstituteinternational.com/organizational-certification/
11. Crisis & Trauma Resources Institute. *Trauma-Informed Leadership*. 2020.

CHAPTER 2

1. "Gartner HR Research Identifies Human Leadership as the Next Evolution of Leadership." Gartner, June 23, 2022. https://www.gartner.com/en/newsroom/press-releases/06-23-22-gartner-hr-research-identifies-human-leadership-as-the-next-evolution-of-leadership
2. S. Hatfield, J. Fisher, and P. Silvergate. "The C-suite's role in well-being." Deloitte. June 22, 2022. https://www2.deloitte.com/us/en/insights/topics/leadership/employee-wellness-in-the-corporate-workplace.html
3. Bryan Robinson. "6 Signs that Quiet Firing Should Be Trending in Your Workplace." *Forbes*, October 1, 2022. https://www.forbes.com/sites/bryanrobinson/2022/10/01/6-signs-that-quiet-firing-could-be-trending-in-your-workplace/
4. P. McGee. "Group of Apple employees pushes back against return-to-office order." *Financial Times*, August 22, 2022. https://www.ft.com/content/e40ba5a2-9dbd-4f88-87f1-c92e412ac132

CHAPTER 3

1. https://cpenneagram.com/centres
2. Sharon K. Ball and Renée Siegel, *Reclaiming You: Using the Enneagram to Move from Trauma to Resilience* (Morgan James Publishing, 2023).

CHAPTER 4

1. *ER*, created by Michael Crichton (1994–2009)
2. Gabor Maté, *The Myth of Normal* (Penguin Random House, 2022).
3. Centre for Mental Health and Addiction (CAMH) *Trauma Overview—Mental Health & Addiction Index*. www.camh.ca

4. Maté, *The Myth of Normal*
5. CTRI Trauma-Informed Care: Building a Culture of Strength Workbook. 2019.
6. Ibid.
7. Bessel van der Kolk, *The Body Keeps the Score: Brain, Mind, and Body in the Healing of Trauma* (Penguin, 2015).
8. Maté, *The Myth of Normal* (quoting Peter Levine)
9. Jennifer Moss, "Burnout Is About Your Workplace, Not Your People." *Harvard Business Review*, December 11, 2019. https://hbr.org/2019/12/burnout-is-about-your-workplace-not-your-people
10. Dr. Dan Siegel, "Dr. Dan Siegel's Hand Model of the Brain" (YouTube) August 9, 2017. https://www.youtube.com/watch?v=f-m2YcdMdFw
11. Ball and Siegel, *Reclaiming You*

CHAPTER 5

1. "How to Help Your Clients Understand Their Window of Tolerance" (blog) *National Institute for the Clinical Application of Behavioral Medicine*. Accessed January 27, 2023. https://www.nicabm.com/trauma-how-to-help-your-clients-understand-their-window-of-tolerance/
2. Deb Dana, *Polyvagal Exercises for Safety and Connection* (WW Norton, 2020).
3. Van der Kolk, *The Body Keeps the Score*
4. Nadine Burke Harris, *The Deepest Well: Healing the Long-Term Effects of Childhood Trauma and Adversity* (Houghton Mifflin Harcourt, 2018).
5. Crisis & Trauma Resources Institute. *Trauma-Informed Leadership*. 2020.
6. Resmaa Menakem. *The Quaking of America: An Embodied Guide to Navigating Our Nation's Upheaval and Racial Reckoning* (Central Recovery Press, 2022).

CHAPTER 6

1. Haruki Murakami. June 22, 2016. (Twitter) https://twitter.com/_harukimurakami/status/745802976938196992?lang=en
2. Brown, *Dare to Lead*
3. Amy Edmondson, "Psychological Safety and Learning Behavior in Work Teams." *Administrative Science Quarterly*, June 24, 2016. https://journals.sagepub.com/doi/abs/10.2307/2666999
4. Brené Brown. Dare to Lead Facilitator Training. San Antonio, Texas. Sept 19, 2019.
5. Tony Schwartz, *The Way We're Working Isn't Working: The Four Forgotten Needs That Energize Great Performance* (Free Press, 2011).
6. The Rise of Workplace Surveillance," *The Daily* (podcast), August 24, 2022. https://www.nytimes.com/2022/08/24/podcasts/the-daily/workplace-surveillance-productivity-tracking.html

CHAPTER 7

1. Benjamin Franklin, "Advice to a Young Tradesman" in *The American Instructor, Or, Young Man's Best Companion.* George Fisher. (1748).
2. "Benjamin Franklin," History.com. Accessed February 14, 2023. https://www.history.com/topics/american-revolution/benjamin-franklin
3. Jessica Stillman, Inc.com. Accessed February 14, 2023. https://www.inc.com/jessica-stillman/for-95-percent-of-human-history-people-worked-15-hours-a-week-could-we-do-it-again
4. Crisis & Trauma Resource Institute, *Trauma-Informed Leadership*. 2020.
5. Marcus Buckingham, *Love and Work: How to Find What You Love, Love What You Do, and Do It for the Rest of Your Life* (Harvard Business Review Press, 2022).

6. "The social enterprise at work: Paradox as a path forward." 2020 Deloitte Global Human Capital Trends. https://www2.deloitte.com/content/dam/Deloitte/at/Documents/human-capital/at-hc-trends-2020.pdf
7. Brown, *Dare to Lead*
8. Burke Harris, *The Deepest Well*
9. Robert Sutton and Ben Wigert, "More Harm Than Good: The Truth About Performance Reviews." Gallup, May 6, 2019. https://www.gallup.com/workplace/249332/harm-good-truth-performance-reviews.aspx?version=prin

CHAPTER 8

1. Ed Schein, *Humble Leadership: The Power of Relationships, Openness, and Trust* (Berrett-Koehler, 2018).
2. David Zes and Dana Landis, "A better return on self-awareness: Companies with higher rates of return on stock also have employees with few personal blind spots." Korn Ferry Institute, August 2013.
3. Debebe, G. (2017). Authentic Leadership and Talent Development: Fulfilling Individual Potential in Sociocultural Context. Advances in Developing Human Resources, 19(4), 420-438. doi:10.1177/1523422317728938
4. Xiong, K., Lin, W., Li, J. C., & Wang, L. (2016). Employee Trust in Supervisors and Affective Commitment. Psychological Reports, 118(3), 829 848. doi:10.1177/0033294116644370
5. Elizabeth Lesser, *Cassandra Speaks: When Women Are the Storytellers, the Human Story Changes* (HarperCollins, 2020).
6. Ibid.

7. Mindfulness and Enneagram Centers of Intelligence, Part 2. Integrative Enneagram Solutions. June 2022.
8. "Gartner HR Research Identifies Human Leadership as the Next Evolution of Leadership." Gartner, June 23, 2022. https://www.gartner.com/en/newsroom/press-releases/06-23-22-gartner-hr-research-identifies-human-leadership-as-the-next-evolution-of-leadership
9. David Rock, "We Need Time to Rehabilitate from the Trauma of the Pandemic." *Harvard Business Review*, February 7, 2022. https://hbr.org/2022/02/we-need-time-to-rehabilitate-from-the-trauma-of-the-pandemic

CHAPTER 9

1. Scott Berinato, "That discomfort you're feeling is grief" *Harvard Business Review*, March 23, 2020. https://hbr.org/2020/03/that-discomfort-youre-feeling-is-grief
2. Pauline Boss, *The Myth of Closure: Ambiguous Loss in a Time of Pandemic and Change* (Norton Professional Books, 2021).
3. Daniel Goleman, "Self-Awareness: The Foundation of Emotional Awareness" (LinkedIn) January 12, 2017. https://www.linkedin.com/pulse/self-awareness-foundation-emotional-intelligence-daniel-goleman/
4. Daniel Goleman, "What Is Emotional Self-Awareness?" Korn Ferry, 2019. https://www.kornferry.com/insights/this-week-in-leadership/what-is-emotional-self-awareness-2019
5. Menakem, *The Quaking of America*

6. Marc Brackett, *Permission to Feel: Unlocking the Power of Emotions to Help Our Kids, Ourselves, and Our Society Thrive* (Celadon, 2019).
7. Susan David, *Emotional Agility: Get Unstuck, Embrace Change, and Thrive in Work and Life* (Avery, 2016).
8. Crisis & Trauma Resource Institute. *Trauma-Informed Leadership*. 2020.
9. Dana, *Polyvagal Exercises for Safety and Connection*
10. Burke Harris, *The Deepest Well*
11. Personal conversation with Uranio Paes. October 27, 2022. Menlo Park, California.

CHAPTER 10

1. Menakem, *The Quaking of America*
2. Burke Harris, *The Deepest Well*
3. Ibid.
4. Ball and Siegel, *Reclaiming You*
5. Ibid.
6. Dana, *Polyvagal Exercises for Safety and Connection*
7. Lesser, *Cassandra Speaks*
8. Menakem, *The Quaking of America*

CHAPTER 11

1. James Clear, *Atomic Habits: An Easy & Proven Way to Build Good Habits & Break Bad Ones* (Avery, 2018).
2. "The Monomyth: (The Hero's Journey): The Hero's Journey," Grand Valley State University, December 9, 2022. https://libguides.gvsu.edu/monomyth

3. "The Monomyth: (The Hero's Journey): The Heroine's Journey," Grand Valley State University, December 9, 2022. https://libguides.gvsu.edu/monomyth

AFTERWORD

1. Thich Nhat Hanh, *Being Peace* (United Buddhist Church, 1987).

YGTMedia Co. is a blended boutique publishing house for mission-driven humans. We help seasoned and emerging authors "birth their brain babies" through a supportive and collaborative approach. Specializing in narrative nonfiction and adult and children's empowerment books, we believe that words can change the world, and we intend to do so one book at a time.

ygtmedia.co/publishing

@ygtmedia.company

@ygtmedia.co

Made in the USA
Las Vegas, NV
18 October 2024

10019047R00134